More advance praise for *Publishing Confidential:*

"If you really want to *publish*—not just write—a nonfiction book, then study and follow what Paul B. Brown has to say. He is a seasoned pro who will unveil the intricacies of the publishing process and give you pragmatic and proven strategies for getting your book to the market it deserves. Trust me on this; he's played a central role getting my books published!"

—James M. Citrin, coauthor of *Lessons from the Top* and *The Five Patterns of Extraordinary Careers;* author of *Zoom*

"A funny, realistic view of the publishing process and a must-read for anyone who thinks he has a book in him. I wish all my clients would read this!"

—Debra Kass Orenstein, literary property attorney

"You're better off not knowing what goes on inside a fine restaurant's kitchen—or a publisher's office. But if you must peer into the pressure-filled, overheated world of books (and remember that there are no health inspectors here), you'll find no better guide than Paul B. Brown. He knows how the sausages are made."

—Marion K. Maneker, publishing columnist for *New York Magazine*

"Paul B. Brown's book will be an enormous help to new authors (and some more experienced ones) who—whether they know it or not—need to understand the inner workings of the nonfiction book business in order to position their projects appropriately. The industry is full of dark pathways, and this book will help writers avoid the obstacles and navigate their way into print."

—Agent Brian DeFiore, DeFiore and Company

"The chapter on marketing alone is worth your next raise. *Publishing Confidential* is a must-read for any executive who wants to get a book published."

—Paul Fargis, Publisher, The Stonesong Press

"Paul B. Brown's book, *Publishing Confidential*, is the Straight Talk Express of the publishing world. To paraphrase Roy Blount's (admittedly bizarre) maxim 'Camels are easy, comedy is hard,' Brown offers: 'Writing is easy, getting published is hard.' But it will be a lot less hard if you read this book. If you want to increase your odds of being published, buy this book."

—Alex Beam, columnist, *The Boston Globe,*
and author of *Gracefully Insane*

"In the real world, there are two kinds of writers: starving artists and successful business people. If you aspire to the latter, this book's for you. Brown's approach is bottom-line oriented, actionable, and effective. Read and prosper!"

—Frank Armstrong, President, Investor Solutions Inc.,
and author of *The Informed Investor*

"As a literary agent I can confirm the fact that if every author would simply read and heed Paul B. Brown's Chapter Five ('Creating the Proposal') and follow his methodology for preparing their own material, there would be many more authors in print today. That one chapter alone is worth the price of admission to the remainder of Brown's excellent 'how to' guide for anyone interested in how publishing really works."

—Stan Wakefield, President, SMW Productions, Inc.

"Brown knows the authoring process from so many angles that he somehow manages to make publishing seem straightforward. Not to mention possible. What he's written isn't just for anyone who's ever wanted to write a book, it's for anyone who's ever read a book and wondered how it got made. Brown pulls back the curtain. Now you can see the wizard for yourself and laugh along the way. This guy is funny. It was the Greeks who first worried about presenting humor and gravity combined—but then, they hadn't read Brown. I have. So should you."

—Michael S. Hopkins, novelist and Editor-at-Large, *Inc.* magazine

Publishing
Confidential

Other books by Paul B. Brown (to show that he may have a clue):

Citizen Investor: How One Word Can Fund Your Retirement (with Phil Dow). RBC Dain Rauscher, 2004.

The Map of Innovation: Creating Something out of Nothing (with Kevin O'Connor). Crown Business, 2003.

Zoom: How 12 Exceptional Companies Are Navigating the Road to the Next Economy (with James M. Citrin). Doubleday, 2001.

Lessons from the Top: The Search for America's Best Business Leaders (with Thomas J. Neff and James M. Citrin). Doubleday, 1999.

The Enneagram Advantage: Putting the 9 Personality Types to Work in the Office (with Helen Palmer). Harmony Books, 1998.

Leading People: Transforming Business from the Inside Out (with Robert H. Rosen). Viking, 1996.

The Corporate Coach: How to Build a Team of Loyal Customers and Happy Employees (with James B. Miller). St. Martin's, 1993.

Grow Rich Slowly: The Merrill Lynch Guide to Retirement Planning (with Don Underwood). Viking, 1993.

My Season on the Brink: A Father's Seven Weeks As a Little League Manager. St. Martin's, 1992.

Customers for Life: How to Turn That One-Time Buyer into a Lifetime Customer (with Carl Sewell). Doubleday, 1990.

Marketing Masters: Lessons in the Art of Marketing from Those Who Do It Best. Harper & Row, 1988.

Sweat Equity: What It Really Takes to Build America's Best Small Companies—By the Guys Who Did It (with Geoffrey N. Smith). Simon and Schuster, 1986.

Publishing Confidential

The Insider's Guide to
What It *Really* Takes to
Land a Nonfiction Book Deal

Paul B. Brown

with illustrations by Britton Payne
and snide editorial comments by
Ellen Kadin, AMACOM Books

AMACOM

American Management Association

New York • Atlanta • Brussels • Chicago • Mexico City • San Francisco
Shanghai • Tokyo • Toronto • Washington, D.C.

This publication is designed to provide accurate and authoritative information in regard to the subject matter covered. It is sold with the understanding that the publisher is not engaged in rendering legal, accounting, or other professional service. If legal advice or other expert assistance is required, the services of a competent professional person should be sought.

Library of Congress Cataloging-in-Publication Data

Brown, Paul B.
    Publishing confidential : the insider's guide to what it really takes to land a nonfiction book deal / Paul B. Brown ; with illustrations by Britton Payne ; and snide editorial comments by Ellen Kadin.
        p.   cm.
    Includes index.
    ISBN 0–8144–7226–5
    1. Authorship—Marketing. 2. Book proposals. I. Title.
PN161.B77 2004
070.5'2—dc22
                                        2003019963

Printing number
10   9   8   7   6   5   4   3   2   1

For Ali,

Because I really wouldn't last
ten minutes without you.

Contents

Foreword

You have just acquired one helluva guide to the process of crafting a proposal, selling it, and ultimately delivering a finished manuscript. Paul B. Brown is an experienced and accomplished pro, and in this book he delivers remarkably smart and pragmatic advice for every wannabe author who wants to put him or herself through the torture of writing a book.

Yes, I mean torture. I've written or coauthored eight books (a half-dozen fewer than Paul), and as a professional writer, author, and editor, I can tell you that there's little I've ever done in this world that is as emotionally exhausting or as mentally taxing as writing a good book. Or, I should add, as intellectually challenging or ego satisfying. A book invites deep and engaged introspection, as well as obsession. It is an all-consuming affair that is as demanding as anything you will ever do. This is Chinese water torture times ten.

That's why I wish I had had access to Paul's wise counsel when I first decided to become an author nearly twenty years ago with a book called *The Headhunters*. It would have made the job so much easier. I've always marveled at Paul's ability to juggle numerous writing projects, including books, with the aplomb of one of those frenetic plate spinners on the Ed Sullivan Show. We met when we were both "the lowliest" staff members at *Forbes* magazine in the early 1980s. Paul was as productive a writer then as he is now. One other fact worth noting: He is one of the least suffering of all the writers I know, which makes him the perfect person to dispense advice to anyone ambitious enough to write a book.

Publishing Confidential gives you the basics with wit, irreverence, simplicity, and good sense. In other words, it's a how-to, tell-it-like-it-is book that delivers the goods. Filled with personal observations and anecdotes, *Publishing Confidential* brings readers behind the scenes of the publishing business and into the mind of an incredibly prolific writer and author. Paul's tale of how a focus group (yes, believe it or not) shaped the writing and editing of one of his early and most successful books, *Customers for Life,* is worth the price of admission alone. So is his two-step litmus test for what you may want to write.

What's new?

Why should anyone care?

Besides, no matter what you do, there can be a rather compelling career reason to write a good book. There's no better calling card or credential for you and what you offer the world. A book instantly confers "expert" status. After my first book was published, I was amazed at how people suddenly thought of me differently. I was no longer a reporter who dashed off a story on a subject. I was now an unqualified authority. Other writers came to me to comment on the business of executive search or on individual players in the industry. The world's largest search firms sought me out to speak at their annual conferences.

A book can be a powerful endorsement of your knowledge or expertise. A few years ago, the magazine I now edit ran a famous cover story written by management guru Tom Peters. It was called "The Brand Called You." The idea was simple: all of us are our own brands. We not only have to invest in ourselves; we have to market ourselves to the world in a way that enriches our brand. If we're to cultivate and nourish our careers, and protect ourselves in a world where there is little loyalty shown to employees by corporations, then we have to market and promote ourselves with the same thought and energy that P&G brings to a soap or a detergent. There are few things that can more effectively help one's brand than a book, even one that never hits the bestseller lists.

But there's something else that is magical about getting a book published under your own name, walking into a bookstore or a library and seeing your book on the shelf, or, even better, sitting in an airplane or a train and watching a stranger read your own words off a page. Here I'm reminded of some wonderful advice a friend gave me. He said he had three goals in life: to plant a tree, to have a son, and to write a book. The ambition in all of us requires that we leave some mark on the world to let others know we lived and we made a difference, however small. I know Paul's sage advice can help many others realize that dream as well.

John A. Byrne
Editor-in-Chief, *Fast Company*
Coauthor of *Jack: Straight from the Gut*

CHAPTER 1

An Introduction of Sorts

"No man but a blockhead ever wrote except for money."
—SAMUEL JOHNSON

"Dr. Johnson was a very smart guy."
—PAUL B. BROWN

A recent Saturday afternoon spent at a bookstore, the Barnes & Noble superstore in suburban New York to be more precise, revealed the following:

○ "I've heard that's a really interesting book" has replaced "What's your sign" as the most popular (failed) pickup line.

○ There is a surefire bestseller to be written called *An Angel Taught Me How to Lose Weight and Have Better Sex . . . And I Want to Share My Secrets with You,* since it would combine two best-selling categories: diet books and those involving metaphysical experiences.

○ There are a large number of "How to Get Your Book Published" books out there.

So why would I want to write another one? Well, there are two practical reasons:

1. AMACOM, the fine publisher that is bringing you this book, asked me to write one.

2. And much more important from your point of view: The ones that are out there neither tell you honestly what the publishing process is like, nor what it actually takes to get your book published.

This one will do both.

Perhaps the easiest way to explain how is to start by talking about what you are not trying to do. You are *not* trying to write a book. (Or, at least, I am not writing a book to help you learn how to write a book.) There is no point.

Anyone can write a book. You sit down and type, or you write something in longhand and get someone to type it for you. Then maybe you get yourself a software program that makes the output look pretty—all the paragraphs are flush left on the page and there are a half-dozen different fonts—and you go down to your local printer and run off a couple of copies and have them professionally bound. And yes, if you go through that process, you have, indeed, written a book.

But publishing that sort of book is not what this book is about.

Now, maybe I am wrong. Maybe that's exactly what you want to do. If it is, go do it. And if you have actually bought this book in the hopes that I can help you create your own special limited-edition book, one destined to be read solely by kith and kin, write me at PaulBBrown@aol.com and I will refund whatever you paid, because I am not going to be of much help to you.

But if you think typing out something and running off a couple of copies that you hand out to family and friends makes you a published author, well, let me introduce you to my little Lithuanian grandmother.

Her English wasn't great and my Lithuanian was lousy, but still Grandma Ruth (a very rough translation of her name in Lithuanian) managed to communicate to me three things about her adopted country.

First, she couldn't believe what a wonderful place it was. The concept of supermarkets—especially those that opened early and closed late—thrilled her every day until she died. She never could get over the variety of items that you could get in one place. She always said the word *supermarket* with an extra emphasis on the first syllable. She made it a point to go to a supermarket daily, even if all she needed was one item.

While other books talk about how to write a book, our focus is on getting you published.

The second thing that awed her every day of the sixty-two years she lived here, after emigrating at age seventeen, was the fact that her kids—and especially her grandkids, like me—literally could grow up to do anything they wanted. That filled her with a sense of joy that literally could make her cry when she talked about the difference between America and the place she had left as a teenager. She couldn't understand why anyone would want to write books for a living when they could "have a real job," but she was still thrilled that her first grandson had the option.

And finally, she couldn't get over the fact that there was a tendency among her newly rich friends to put on airs.

Upon reaching age sixty, one of them bought a fourteen-foot boat that was little more than a rowboat with a motor, but to hear him go on about it—in *his* heavily Lithuanian-accented English—you might have thought it was the second coming of the *Queen Mary*, as opposed to something that could barely circumnavigate Coney Island. To underscore the fact that he was now a true salt, he bought a blue blazer and white duck pants and took to wearing a naval commander's hat on weekends.

My grandmother's reaction? "He may think he's a captain, but to real captains, he is no captain."[1]

To paraphrase Grandma Ruth, if you write a book whose entire print run consists of the couple of copies you make for family and friends, or worse, one that ends up sitting in your desk drawer forever, you are no author.[2]

In writing a book, what you really want to do is get it published, and published properly—that is, with a large first printing, advertising and marketing support from the publisher, and a decent amount of money up front.

Since I truly believe that, let me be brutally honest:

I think it is a bad idea to begin writing a book unless you know that someone is going to publish it.

You don't want to devote a substantial part of your life creating 300 or 400 or 500 double-spaced pages only to discover that no one wants to pay you for what you have written. Not only is it demoralizing, it ends up being a huge waste of time.

You'll want to discover if you have a potential audience before you invest a lot of time. (That is something we will be talking about in Chapter 2 and Chapter 3.)

So, yes, this book has a definitely commercial slant. That, to me, makes it different from the books already out there—as do its approach, tone, and how-to content.

Let's talk about the approach first.

---

1. And every time he came to visit, she took to cursing him under her breath in Lithuanian. The literal translation of the curse was: "May he grow like a turnip with his head in the ground," but that is another matter.

2. Now, going down to Kinko's and running off five copies is far different from the concept of *professionally* self-publishing, where you write a book, usually for an extremely targeted audience, and then act as your own publisher instead of signing on with the Simon & Schusters, Doubledays, and AMACOMs of this world. If you have the right content targeted for a specific niche, this may be exactly the way to go.

We are going to talk about this in Chapter 9. But to foreshadow that discussion: If the market for what you have is relatively small, or you are predominantly publishing a book as a marketing tactic—either for yourself or your business—then self-publishing a couple of thousand books and selling them yourself can make an awful lot of sense.

The Importance of Not Being Earnest

It seems to me that the focus of most of the how-to-get-a-book-published books is completely backward. These books spend the majority of the time—and majority can be upward of 90 percent—on how to write the book and very little time on how to get it published.

Our book will take the opposite approach. After all, it always struck me that Dr. Johnson got it right in the quote that kicked off this chapter: "No man but a blockhead ever wrote except for money."

So our assumption is fourfold. You:

(a) Are not a blockhead.

(b) Have something to say.

(c) Know how to say it. That means we are going to spend no time on how to put together a simple declarative sentence or different approaches to writing or whether it is best to have soft classical music playing in the background as you write.

(d) Want to create your book as efficiently as possible. That means:

   ○ You are not going to create excuses ("I just don't have the time") that allow you to put off what you want to say.

   ○ You want the process of getting published to move quickly and be friction-free to the extent humanly possible.

All this leaves us free to concentrate on how you can best publish what you create. And that brings us to the question of tone.

I always get the impression I should be reading the competing books in church or during a break in the High Holy Days services at the neighborhood temple. They are earnest beyond belief.

That's fine, I guess, but it doesn't reflect the reality of the audience. The vast majority of the people—and I assuming that this includes you—who buy these books already have a day job. (More on that in a minute.) You want to be published, but you won't die if it doesn't happen. Creating a book is important to you, sure, but you have some perspective on what you are trying to do; and rumor has it, you have a sense of humor.

And, I am assuming, you want practical information that you can put to use immediately.

That's exactly what you are going to get. Here's a quick example. If you want to find an agent, the traditional advice is to do the following:

○ Get an agent directory, which is nothing more than a book that lists every literary agent out there and gives a sketchy idea of what kind of books they represent—novels, business books, whatever.

○ Write the prettiest pitch letter you can, describing what you want to sell.

○ Send the same letter out to everyone in the directory asking each agent to represent you and your idea.

○ Keep your fingers crossed.

How does this approach work? Not very well. My agent, Rafe Sagalyn, is listed in all the agent directories. He gets—by actual count—about 100 letters and/or e-mails a month from people who have read the traditional advice, write him explaining their idea for a book, and ask if he would like to represent them.

Listen to him explain what happens then. "Out of the 1,200 letters and pitches I get each year, I sign up about four people."

The typical advice—get an agent directory, write the prettiest pitch letter you can, and send it out to everyone who could conceivably be interested—is not helpful. In my agent's case, it gives you a 1-in-300 chance of success.

Here's what our response is to the question, "Can you give me a list of good agents?"

Without knowing in detail what you want to write, who your market is, how you plan to address it—that is, all the questions your proposal (see Chapter 5) will answer—a list of agents won't help you much.

Some are better at some things than others.

The easiest thing to do? Follow a simple three-step process: (a) pick up a couple of books that are similar to the one you plan to write, (b) see who the author thanks as his or her agent, and (c) write that agent.

That way you are:

○ *Dealing with a qualified agent. (He sold a book.)*

○ *Writing to someone who has an interest in your topic. (He sold a book on the same topic you want to write about.)*

Obviously, our approach requires more work. You have to go beyond the directory's listing that "Rafe Sagalyn sells nonfiction books" to learn he has a passion for new management ideas. But it is far more effective than sending out letters at random.

This is the kind of advice you are going to find throughout this book. If you are looking for a book that talks about "the inner joy you will get from writing" or how the publication of your book will fill you with the same sense of wonder as you get from the birth of a child, you'd be better off somewhere else.

Bragging on Myself

At this point, it is probably worth explaining who I am and why you should believe anything I have to say about any of this.

I've been writing books for twenty years. As the list at the beginning of the book shows, I have done them for just about all the major publishers, and, perhaps more important, I have an impressively *uneven* track record of success.

I have written books such as *Sweat Equity,* which disappeared without a trace, and some such as *Customers for Life,* which have been disgustingly successful. (That book is still out there in hardcover, and there have been two updated versions of the paperback over the years.)

I think the range of sales is important. If everything I had written bombed, I'd have zero credibility. If everything was a smash, I wouldn't have learned much about the publishing process.

I have learned a lot. Much of it the hard way. As the old lyric goes, "Things I haven't learned at first, I learned by doing twice."

And maybe some of what I've learned can help you.

So if you are looking for a practical, how-to approach to getting your book published, you have come to the right place.

It occurred to me that if I promised you an insider's account of what it takes to land a book deal, it would be helpful to hear from someone actually capable of writing the check. That's why, throughout, you will read editorial asides from Ellen Kadin, my acquisitions editor at AMACOM. Ellen is an industry veteran. More important, she is bright and funny—alas, often at my expense. Her comments will always be introduced by "E.K.:". Pay attention to what she has to say.

Let's get to work.

CHAPTER 2

"What Do You Have; Why Should I Care?" Asks Your Potential Publisher

Sex always hooks people's attention, so let's begin this chapter by talking about sex.

Not that long ago, one of the leading women's magazines noticed that a lot of their readers were reporting that they were hungry after making love, so the magazine commissioned a study to find out why.

The hope? That the act itself was responsible for burning off lots of calories and the magazine could do an article entitled "How to Lose Lots of Weight While Having Lots of Great Sex!"

(My interest in the article wasn't prurient, just practical. Someone—that is, me—might be able to turn the article into a book.)

The researchers went out and surveyed a statistically valid sample of women to find out what was causing this potentially weight-reducing reaction.

And what was the number-one reason women were hungry after having sex?

They had been hungry before they had sex.

Honest.

Sometimes, the most obvious answer is the one that is most overlooked.

It is no different when you are trying to get a book published: It is easy, for example, to skip right over the fact that you need to be able to:

(a) Explain your idea clearly

(b) Make it instantly obvious why the world needs to hear what you have to say

If you ignore either step, you may never get your book published. By the time you finish reading this chapter, there should be no danger of that.

"Remember When . . ."

Everyone likes to think they were working during the golden age of their industry or profession. For television writers it was the 1950s, when everything from *I Love Lucy* to *The Adventures of Ozzie and Harriet* set the tone for what would follow for the next fifty years.

For the makers of bell-bottoms and platform shoes, and the people who raise polyesters, it was the 1970s; and for business writers, it was probably the 1980s. (The fact that I was a writer and editor for national business magazines [*Business Week* and *Forbes*] during the decade is merely a coincidence.)

Three interrelated things happened back then to make business journalism hot for the first time since Guttenberg combined the concepts of the wine press and the coin stamper to create the printing press in the fifteenth century.

First, the stock market finally recovered from the horrific bear market of 1972 to 1973. The Dow Jones Industrial Average just about tripled during the 1980s.

Second, companies started switching from defined benefit plans (pensions) to defined contributions to employee retirement accounts (401k's and their nonprofit equivalents), forcing people (you and me) to make their own investment decisions, which spurred the demand for financial information of all types.

If you want publishers to say "yes," you need to explain what's in it for them.

Third, baby boomers, who have a disproportionate amount of influence over everything (just given their size—there are 76 million of them) were starting to enter the management ranks, which, by definition (in their eyes), made writing about management important. (It is no coincidence that just about every major newspaper began beefing up its business coverage at this time.)

If you were at a major business magazine in the 1980s, things couldn't get much better. Ad pages were soaring, so you had all the space you needed to tell a story; no one looked too closely at your expense account; and even the lowliest staff writer (who would have been me at *Forbes* in 1981) had CEOs coming to their office every couple of hours basically pleading for coverage of their companies.

One day over lunch, a couple of the reporters tried to figure out what would be the most efficient line of questioning to get the CEOs—and their attendant retinue of public relations people and various and sundry toadies—out of our offices so that we could do something productive (such as trying to turn one of our articles into a book).

We finally figured out that we could reduce everything we needed to find out about a company to two questions:

1. What do you have? (In other words, "What's new?")

2. Why should I (as a surrogate for our readers) care?

Yes, these questions were remarkably snotty **[E.K.: Not for you they're not.]**, but they really get to the heart of the matter—both in journalism and in figuring out if your book idea has merit.

Step #1: Explaining What You've Got

Remember our basic premise. You aren't trying to write a book; you are trying to get your book published.

Well, the first step in doing that is being able to explain what you have *in a simple, declarative sentence*. Clearly, if you get that far, and someone is potentially interested, you will be able to explain your idea in a 6,000- to 10,000-word proposal that you create for your book. (See Chapter 5.)

But nobody is ever going to ask you for a proposal unless you initially can explain to an editor or agent your book idea *in a single sentence.*

This is a concept I borrowed from my friend Kevin O'Connor, who has helped start countless companies—DoubleClick and Flex-Play among them. Kevin's theory is as simple as it is sound: If you can't explain in a single sentence what your company/product/service/book idea does (or will do), then nobody will understand what you have.

In other words, if they don't "get it" quickly, they won't get it at all.

And you won't have the time to explain it to them. No one will let you. Everyone's busy. People don't have the time to sit down and listen to an hour-long spiel about your book idea. They don't have a half hour to give you. They won't even give you five minutes. So you have to tell them quickly, in one sentence. [**E.K.: Did you need this many sentences to get your point across?**]

You can always go further—if the potential publisher, editor, or agent is willing to let you. But you need to have your positioning reduced to a sentence, just in case they aren't willing to spend the time—and they probably won't be.

Is this unfair?

Yes.

Now, get over it.

Authors, and especially would-be authors, fall in love with their ideas. And they should. They are devoting big hunks of their lives to them.

But it is simply naive to expect that everyone else on the planet is going to share your enthusiasm. They aren't going to care.

I can brag about my kids all day, but it didn't take me long to realize after my firstborn arrived that not everyone wanted to see all the baby pictures I had taken. People have their own projects and agendas (and kids). That's why you have to tell them what you've got in a sentence. [**E.K.: Don't give them any ideas. What editor wants a query consisting solely of "what the book is about"? Tell them to read Chapter 5.**]

It's easy to fill a full page—or even the thirty to fifty of them that will make up a book proposal—with what your book is about. It's far tougher to put it into a single, coherent, *basic* sentence.

How basic? Think "subject + verb + object." That basic, that focused.

Here are real examples from books I've pitched successfully:

- ○ "Customer service can be a business strategy." (*Customers for Life*)

- ○ "What Peters and Waterman did with big companies, with *In Search of Excellence,* we want to do here with small companies." (*Sweat Equity*)

- ○ "I want to take an in-depth look at six of the best marketing companies on the planet—according to me, the [then] marketing editor of *Business Week.*" (*Marketing Masters*)

- ○ "I want to tell the world how nuts I became coaching my seven-year-old in Little League." (*My Season on the Brink*)

Is it difficult to reduce what is going to be a 200-, 300-, or 400-page book into a single sentence? You bet. But you have no choice. People aren't willing to listen to much more than that from me when I pitch my books—either then or now—and they are not going to be willing to listen to all that much more from you.

Besides, reducing your idea to one sentence forces you to really focus hard on what you are trying to say, and it turns out to be a pretty good litmus test. Again, if you can't explain your book in one sentence, then you may not have a good handle on what it is you are trying to sell.

In one of my first assignments at *Forbes,* I was given one magazine page—and that included the headline and a photo—to do the definitive corporate profile on Exxon. When I complained to editor James W. Michaels that I needed more space to talk about what was going on at what was then the world's largest company, his response was to the point: "If you can't write about Exxon in 800 words, then you don't know what the story is."

To paraphrase Michaels, if you can't define your book in a sentence, how can you expect an agent or editor to understand what you have?

Step #2: Why Should Anyone Care?

Of course, you can reduce your idea to a crystal clear sentence, but if no one is interested, you are not going to get published—unless you publish it yourself. And even then, nobody is going to read it.

That's why you need to explain why a reader should care about what you want to say.

It is lovely that you want to tell your tender coming-of-age story or chronicle the twists and turns of your forty years in the paper clip industry. But people hearing your idea are going to have one overarching question: What's in it for me?

They may not be that blunt. But you can be sure that the question will be uppermost in their minds as they read or hear about your idea.

That's why you need to answer the question: Why should a publisher (as surrogate for the reader) care about what you are pitching? If the reader doesn't care, he or she isn't going to buy the book. And if no one is going to buy the book, the publisher has no reason to bring it out (or pay you for writing it.)

[E.K.: Cheer up. You can reuse this material in the annoying book-marketing questionnaire that your publisher will insist that you complete later.]

Let's go back to the four ideas for books that we discussed a second ago, and let me show you how I tried to answer the "What's in it for me (the publisher/reader)" question.

○ Customer service is a business strategy. (*Customers for Life*) What's in it for the reader? "They can make more money, if they treat their customers correctly, and we will provide dozens of examples of what 'correctly' means and how they can do it."

○ What Peters and Waterman did with big companies, with *In Search of Excellence,* we want to do with small companies. (*Sweat Equity*) What's in it for the reader? "By studying and then implementing the 'best practices' of leading small firms, companies of all sizes can benefit."

○ I want to take an in-depth look at six of the best marketing companies on the planet—according to me, the [then] marketing editor of *Business Week.* (*Marketing Masters*) The rationale for my second book was basically the same as it was for *Sweat Equity,* my first. I was still new to book writing and didn't want to stray far from what had worked the first time.

○ I want to tell the world how nuts I became coaching my seven-year-old in Little League. (*My Season on the Brink*) What's in it for the reader? "On one level, it is a cautionary tale about what can happen to naturally competitive people in a situation that is supposed to be fun. On another, it is just a purely entertaining read."

Hedging Your Bets

Please alert the heresy police. The following section violates how purists think a book should be created.

It does so for two reasons:

1. The traditionalists are wrong.

2. I've discovered that what follows dramatically increases the chances of getting your book published, which is the point of this entire exercise.

Let's go back to something we said earlier: You need to explain how your book will benefit the reader because publishers are only interested in bringing out books that will sell.

But how do you know readers will benefit?

Most of the time, potential and published authors answer the question based on instinct. They say things like: "I think they will be interested in this topic because . . ."

And sometimes they answer by placing themselves in the position of the reader. "I know I would like to read a book about XYZ, and so that is the kind of book I am going to write."

Both those approaches are fine, but they can be improved—perhaps dramatically—by shifting the point of view. Here's a thought: If you want to know if people are interested in what your book is about, ask them.

Let me give you an example.

The $332,000 Customer

Back in 1988, I wrote a story for *Inc.* magazine on what it was like to be an entrepreneur who suddenly found himself or herself to be a celebrity as well. I talked to Debbie Fields (Mrs. Fields of Mrs. Fields' cookies) and a handful of other entrepreneurs who were getting a lot of press as entrepreneurship moved to center stage in the business community (and in the business press).

As part of the piece, I talked to the man who was then (and is now) the country's largest luxury car dealer.

Carl Sewell and I hit it off, and a few months later, when I was thinking about doing a customer service book, I figured Carl would be the perfect person to partner with. All his dealerships—whether they offer Chevys or Infinitis—sell on service, not price, and any car dealer who has an excellent reputation for service had to be someone I could learn from.

We got together, convinced Doubleday to give us some money, and set off to write a book that had a then radical message: that customer service can be a business strategy. I knew just what to call it: *The*

$332,000 Customer. The title, I thought, was intriguing, just the thing to make a book jump off the business shelf.

The title came from the amount of money that one of Carl's customers, on average, spends with him over the course of his or her lifetime. I was thrilled with the title and our approach, which called for dividing the book into eight aspects of customer service and showing readers how they could implement each one of them profitably.

We were about three-quarters of the way done when Carl, who had never written a book before, asked what he thought was the world's most basic question: "When are we going to show a focus group what we have?"

Focus *what?*

Book publishers never conduct focus groups on individual books, citing the expense, which these days can easily top $25,000 to do well.

But cutting that kind of corner is just stupid, as Carl Sewell was quick to explain politely. How are you ever going to know what a reader wants, unless you ask her?

The answer that comes back from writers and editors is that based on their experience they can act as a surrogate for the readers. And I think that is true, to some extent.

But the reality is that relying on an editor's or writer's opinion of what a reader wants is relying on secondhand information. It is almost always better to go to the source. If you want to know what potential book buyers think about what you have, it is best to ask them directly.

Doubleday was not about to pay for a focus group, so Carl did. He hired Yankelovich, a major research firm, and told the firm to assemble a representative group of people likely to read our book. The requirements were that:

1. They had to have read at least four out of a list of twelve business bestsellers that had been published in the previous year, with one of the titles being a book by Tom Peters. (Tom, who was reaching his peak as a business guru at about that time, was going to write our introduction.)

2. They must hold a senior management position or be the head of their own company.

Yankelovich found a dozen people who met the criteria and agreed to participate; we sent each of them the first 100 manuscript pages of the book and gave them a week to take a look. Then we all gathered in a Yankelovich office in Connecticut. The twelve people—eight men, four women—sat around a conference table with a moderator, while Carl, Harriet Rubin, our editor at Doubleday, and I sat on the other side of a one-way mirror. (The participants were told we were listening and watching. As you will see, it did not inhibit them one whit.)

After some preliminary small talk, the moderator began: "By now you have all read the first part of a book that Doubleday will be publishing in the spring, and I'd like to talk a little bit about your reaction to it. Let's start with the title, *The $332,000 Customer.* What do you think?"

There was a little bit of general discussion and it quickly became clear that the group was split. Nine of the twelve people thought it was absolutely the worst title they had ever heard. The other three said they had heard worse.

"What didn't you like about it?" asked the moderator.

MAN #1: "It was confusing; it didn't mean anything."

MAN #2: "The number in the title makes it sound like the book only deals with retailers selling really expensive items, those that cost $332,000, but when you read the text it is clear that it applies to every business, even mine. But I am not a retailer, and if I wasn't being paid to read the text, I would have never picked up the book."

WOMAN #1: "The title sounds like you are going to be picking up a novel, instead of a business book."

Yes, everyone had read the chapter where we explained how a customer can easily spend $332,000 with Carl over the course of his or her lifetime, and no, no one cared that we explained where the title came from in the text. The consensus? It was a truly awful title.

"Well, what would you call it?" the moderator asked.

The reaction around the conference table confirmed something that marketing people have known forever about focus groups. Customers and potential customers can give you the attributes they want in a new product, but they never can quite envisage the product itself.

Let's pretend it is the late 1950s, and you want to create a better casual restaurant/diner. If you had convened a focus group, people would have told you some of the things they would like the restaurant to provide: better food, faster service, cleaner surroundings. But never in 10,000 years would they have given you the concept of McDonald's.

It was no different in critiquing the book. The focus group knew, for example, what it didn't like about the title—it was confusing at best and misleading at worst—but the twelve men and women could not agree on what it should be called, but they were very clear about the idea that the title should get across:

"It's about creating lifetime customers."

"How you can hold onto someone who buys from you forever."

"Turning browsers into buyers."

"How you keep a customer forever."

They weren't much more helpful when it came to other parts of the book. The writing, they said, was fine, but couldn't we reorganize things *somehow* to make information easier to use? (They weren't sure how.) They liked the idea of a checklist at the end of the chapter, but couldn't we present it in such a way that they could read it and immediately implement it? (No, they weren't sure how to do that either, but they were clear that we should "make it easy.")

If we gave them a specific question, such as, did they like the idea of more short chapters as opposed to fewer longer ones, they could be specific. (Shorter was better.) But when it came to something they didn't like, be it in terms of content or presentation, they were not clear how to fix it.

For example, at each of Carl Sewell's dealerships a customer service representative is someone who advises you about what is covered by your car's warranty and what is not. This person can also explain the maintenance schedules recommended by the manufacturer.

To everyone in the focus group, though, a customer service rep was someone you had to deal with when something went wrong, or it was another name for a salesperson. No, the group had no idea what the service rep should be called, but "you can't call the guy a customer service rep. It's stupid."

Reacting to All This

The reaction to all these comments was fascinating. Harriet Rubin, who was the hot nonfiction editor at the time, grew more livid with each and every comment the group made during the ninety-minute session. Nobody had questioned her editorial judgment in years. Who were these people finding fault with her work, work that consistently landed two or three of her books on the bestseller lists at any given time? Harriet thought what we had written was fine and that the people Yankelovich had found were dolts.

Carl alternated between staring straight through the one-way glass mirror as if he were watching a car wreck and mumbling, "Didn't they like anything?" The fact that everyone seemed to have a horror story to tell about their local car dealership, and inferred that his places had to be just as bad, did nothing to reduce his blood pressure, which seemed to steadily climb throughout the evening.

And me? Well, no one likes to be criticized, and I thought we had written a pretty good book. But, these were potential book purchasers—people who had the God-given ability to help put my kids through college by buying our book—and they weren't dumb. So, I swallowed hard and tried to think of them collectively as being one cranky magazine editor, and reacted accordingly.

I took lots of notes. I wasn't so much trying to take down every word; I was searching for themes or patterns.

For example:

○ *It was clear we needed a new title.* What kept resonating was that the focus group thought—correctly—that the entire book was about capturing and then keeping a customer forever. Since the fundamental idea was so important to them, we ended up using it twice within the final title, *Customers for Life: How to Turn That One-Time Buyer into a Lifetime Customer.*

○ *Everyone liked the idea of callouts* (bold text within grey boxes throughout the manuscript that highlighted points)[1] *and checklists.*

So we made sure they were present in every chapter.

> **They looked like this and amplified the text.**

○ *Simple is better.* We would go back to find places where one large chapter could be carved into a few smaller ones. Some chapters ended up being just one book page long.

○ *Short sentences, active words.* It was clear that our potential readers were not looking for great literature or memorable phrases, so in the revisions when there was a choice of going with a long, flowing Faulkneresque sentence or a simple declarative one that contained a how-to tip, it was no contest. The *USA Today* approach triumphed over the *New Yorker* every time.

○ *Writing must be painfully clear.* No jargon. Nothing ambiguous. For example, the term *customer service rep*, which had confused some people, was changed to *service advisor* by the time the book went to press.

---

1. Note: The term *callout* is technically used to mean an instruction telling where to place a figure, table, or other element. It has also come to be used by magazine and book writers somewhat informally in the sense I use it here.

We kept the focus group's comments in mind, as we set about revising the book dramatically. The end product was a tightly focused book that argued (apparently convincingly) that customer service is a business strategy and provided tactics that would allow anyone to put that strategy into practice.

Nearly fifteen years later, the book continues to sell well. The moral: Get as much input from potential readers as you can.

Now does this mean you should focus group your idea? In an ideal world, sure. But you don't have to take it that far. [**E.K.: That's good, Paul, since we don't all have $25,000 to spend on focus groups.**] You could:

o Send your table of contents and a chapter or two to members of your trade association or people you know at competing firms. Ask them what you should add or take out.

o Send an e-mail, along with some of the text you have written, to fifty people who might be potential buyers and ask them to comment on specific elements. (Is this too long? Wordy? Too basic? Whatever.)

o Ask your local bookstore to hand out a sample chapter to people who buy similar books and ask both the bookstore owner and the buyers of other books for their help. (You'd be surprised how often they will give it to you.)

Sure, by all means show what you have written to your significant other and friends and family. But with all deference, their opinions are less important. You aren't going to make them buy the final product, and they are predisposed to like you. What you are looking for here are objective comments.

But Is It Art?

Now, purists will tell you that the approach we took in creating *Customers for Life* is the wrong way to go. (Need proof that they think it was wrong? Almost no one uses focus groups for books to this day. Publishers scoff at the idea, saying it is redundant—they know what's best—and too expensive.)

Editors and writers will go on at length about how a book needs to be the translation of *your* vision, and if you are shaping your book based on what others are telling you, it is not your vision. They say if you take this approach, you are "pandering," or reducing what you have to say to the "lowest common denominator." **[E.K.: Do nonfiction editors with a modicum of marketing sense really say this? If an author wants to invest in the kind of market research that will ensure his or her approach resonates with readers in a way that might compel them to buy the book in *droves*, I, for one, will not likely be inclined to discourage such behavior. (But of course I'm not going to pay for it.)]**

Hogwash.

Remember our premise. You are not just trying to create a book. You are trying to create a book that someone will want to publish. And the only way anyone is going to want to publish what you have to say is if you create something that people want to read.

It just seems to me that if you want to know what people want to read, you should ask them and tailor your offering accordingly—if you think their comments make sense.

That last phrase is important.

It's your book. It's your book. It's your book.

People can tell you that your book about the history of fountain pens should include pictures of hot babes (or hunky guys, or both) and you don't think it should, since your focus is on the different materials and designs that have been employed through the years. What do you do? Well, you have the final say. You are not required to include photos from *Baywatch*.

But if you are writing a service book—as we were with what eventually became known as *Customers for Life*—and potential readers tell you the title is awful, they want more callouts and checklists, and they wouldn't mind if the book were completely modular so they could concentrate on the stuff that they thought would help them and be able to skip everything else, then you might want to listen.

We did.

As Carl Sewell told me at the end of the focus group, when we were scrambling to find anything positive that had come out of the experience: "If the dogs won't eat the dog food, it is bad dog food."

While I don't think I would have drawn the analogy between potential readers and dogs as closely as he did **[E.K.: Yes, I believe you would.]**, he's absolutely right. (Carl's attitude may also explain how he was able to build one sleepy car dealership in Dallas into a $1 billion company.)

The opinion of the people who might buy the book is ultimately the one that matters, if you are in this book-writing thing as more than a hobby. That's why we tailored the book as much as we did in response to what the focus group told us. Was it pandering? No. It was simply an attempt to respond to customers' needs.

Did it make the book better?

Absolutely.

I say that from a writing point of view: The book is more, well, focused than it would have been without the focus group—and it definitely improved its sales. Since being published in 1990, *Customers for Life* has been updated and revised twice and has sold about 1 million copies worldwide (with about half of that coming from overseas sales; the book has been translated into sixteen languages).

Asking people what they want to read is a good idea.

Once you have an idea that you can express clearly—and have an answer to the question "What's in it for the reader?"—you are under way.

The next step is to find out if anyone is interested.

CHAPTER 3

Making Contact

Unless you are planning to distribute the book yourself—an option that is discussed in detail in Chapter 9—you need to figure out how you are going to make contact with an editor at one of the traditional publishing houses, the Random Houses, AMACOMs, Berrett-Koehlers, Vikings, and Harvard Business School Presses of the world.

You can do it. Or an agent can do it for you. (There is more information about agents in the second half of this chapter.) But it has to be done. You need an editor interested in your book idea if it is ever going to be something more than an idea.[1]

So, how do you make contact? The short answer: Any way you can.

---

1. As we will talk about later on, having the editor interested is just the starting point. Editors don't have the ability to write you a check. They need to get the approval of their editorial board, which is made up of representatives of not only the editorial department but also the business and marketing sides of the publishing house.

But you are never going to come to the attention of the editorial board unless you initially get an editor interested in what you have. And you are never going to get him interested unless he knows you exist. So, you need to make contact.

But before we start expanding on that answer, and giving you specific steps you can follow, let's begin with what is absolutely the wrong approach to take, if only to make sure you head off in the right direction.

How to Guarantee Your Book Will Never Be Published: A Primer on What Not to Do

Step 1. With no input at all from potential book buyers to tell you what they would want to see in your book (See Chapter 2), sit down and write the complete manuscript, spending months—if not years—on the project.

Step 2. Once you are finished, head down to your local print shop and have fifty copies printed.

Step 3. Overnight the manuscript to "The Editorial Department" at the first fifty publishers you can think of.

Step 4. Sit back and wait for the telephone to ring and the checks to start flowing in.

If you follow Steps 1, 2, 3, and 4, I guarantee that you are never going to get your book published.

We've already talked about why it is a bad idea to write a complete nonfiction book before knowing whether anyone is interested in publishing it,[2] so let's start with Step 2: *Head down to your local print shop and have fifty copies printed.*

What's wrong with that? Well, the first problem of course is the expense. [E.K.: Not always best as the prime consideration; I once had an author who submitted his complete manuscript on 3" by 5" index cards. It was cheap, but not effective.] But the bigger problem is

2. If you are writing *fiction*, you have to write the entire book, or close to it, so that a would-be editor can get a sense of style and plot. But we aren't talking about fiction. I don't know how to write a novel, and I am not going to pretend I know how to sell one. Nonfiction books, as we will discuss in Chapter 5, can be sold on the basis of a proposal, and overwhelmingly are.

While it's a perilous voyage, you *can* make effective contact with a publisher.

that there may not be fifty publishers in the universe who are right for what you have written.

Say you have written the definitive biography of Cletus Leroy Boyer, who played professional baseball in virtual obscurity between 1955 and 1971. Clete Boyer (pronounced BOYer, not like [Charles] BoyYEA, the French movie star of *Gaslight* and *Love Affair*) is best known—if he is known at all—as a member of the 1961 New York Yankees, clearly one of the greatest baseball teams of all time.

But as you go through the Yankees starting nine from that year, there is no doubt that Boyer was their weakest link. The terrific-fielding third baseman was out on the field because of his glove and not his bat. He hit just .224—awful, but only just slightly below his lifetime average of .242.

And on a team where it seemed even the bat boy had 20 home runs—the team as a whole hit 240 homers that year or about 1.5 per game—Boyer banged out just 11 in the 148 games he played.

In short, he was not a star. And unless you were a fan—like me (when I was a kid I desperately wanted to grow up and play third base for the New York Yankees because of Boyer)—you'd have little interest in the biography. I have a signed Clete Boyer baseball sitting on my desk. But I never worry about it being stolen. Who, other than me, would want it?

And publishers are likely to ask who, other than me, is likely to read a Clete Boyer biography?

As we talked about in Chapter 2, publishers are surrogates for their readers. And if the vast majority of the universe has no interest in a Clete Boyer biography, then mass market publishers (e.g., Doubleday, HarperCollins), who try to appeal to most of the universe with their offerings, are not going to have any interest either.

Neither will the publishers who do only fiction, since we are talking about a biography here, nor the people who run the academic or scientific presses. In short, there probably aren't fifty potential publishers of the book. (Heck, there may not even be one.) If you send your Clete Boyer biography to the first fifty publishers you can think of, you are just wasting your time and money.

But you are a stubborn sort, so you move to Step 3: *Overnight the manuscript to "The Editorial Department" at the first fifty publishers you can think of.*

Here's what happens when you do that.

Sometime the next morning your package shows up at the publisher's office. Seeing that it is not addressed to anyone in particular, someone in the mailroom brings the package to a common area near where all the editors work and dumps it with all similar packages into what is referred to as the slush pile.

What happens next depends on the publishing house. At some houses, the packages sit there unopened until the pile gets too big and then they are all thrown away, never to be acknowledged. At others, the packages are eventually opened by an intern, or lowest-ranking member in the department, part of whose job is to send out a rejection letter—which, to add insult to injury, is frequently preprinted. The message goes something like this:

> Thank you so much for your recent submission. Unfortunately, it does not meet our editorial needs at this time.
> We wish you luck in finding an appropriate publisher.

Sometimes they send you your manuscript back, sometimes they don't. But in either case, it is almost never read.[3]

In the rarest of cases, say one time out of fifty, a bored editorial assistant—these are bright young people who are forced to spend at least a year of their working lives as glorified secretaries as part of the learning process of becoming an editor—will actually read something in the slush pile.

[E.K.: Ahem. Paul, I believe you're forgetting that here at AMA-COM it really *is* the editor who will review your submission and decide whether to pursue it. (But I'll concede we're probably an exception.)]

And from the once-in-a-blue-moon category, they may actually like something enough to bring it to their boss. Success in the offing, right? Nope. In those rare cases, the editor usually will give it a quick skim and then reject it. Yes, maybe once in a millennium she may like what she reads enough to take it to the editorial board, which will actually consider the book for publication. But if I had to quantify the odds of something making it from the slush pile to the bookstore, I would put them well north of 10,000:1.

So, sending your book to "The Editorial Department" is not the way to go. And it explains why Step 4: *Sit back and wait for the telephone to ring and the checks to start flowing in* will never happen. Folks aren't going to call and there are not going to be any checks because no one will have read what you sent. That may not be right, but that is the way it is.

You need a better course of action.

---

3. This is something generation after generation of potential authors has learned the hard way.

Invariably, as a test, people who want to be published invert one of the pages in the manuscript they send out as a check to see if someone has read their work. Their expectation is that if they get their book back and page 87 (or whatever) is turned right side up, then at least they know someone took a look at what they sent. Most often they discover that if the manuscript is returned along with the standard-issue rejection letter—and it isn't always—page 87 is still upside down.

The Right Way to Go

At the very least, you need a name, someone you can contact directly. It would be fantastic if it turned out through a terrific twist of fate that your next-door neighbor just happened to be the head of publishing for the house that is perfect for your book. But since the odds of that occurring are about the same as having your book pulled off the slush pile and thrust upon the bestseller list, you need a strategy that is based on more than just blind luck.

Let's begin with the obvious and then move toward the subtle as we go about figuring out the easiest way for you to make direct contact with someone who could publish your book.

We begin at the beginning. What was it that got you thinking about writing a book in the first place? Encouragement from a college science or business professor? If he has written books, you have a place to start. Who was the editor, the agent, who does he know?

Were you inspired by something a colleague said? If so, has she been published? Does this colleague or your marketing or public relations departments have any contacts? How about your trade association? (This book, for example, is from the publishing arm of the American Management Association.)

From there, I'd move on to Aunt Sally. Or maybe cousin Jeff, or the guy you see once a year at the office Christmas party. I can almost guarantee that someone you know knows someone in publishing. Call it six degrees of separation. If you ask enough people, someone will know someone who has either written a book or works for a publishing company.

If that person knows an author, get the author's telephone number or e-mail address and make contact. Ask who this author's editor and agent are (more on that in a second). Get names.

Everyone knows someone who knows someone who knows someone in publishing. If worst comes to worst, network until you find an "in."

Now, common sense is still required. If the writer that your second cousin's hairdresser's boyfriend knows writes Harlequin romances, and you are doing the definitive work on cold fission, then the romance writer's editor is not right for you. But her agent could be, or her husband's sister who publishes book on quarks. Take the connection as far as you can.[4]

Don't limit yourself to people directly associated with the editorial department. If you get the name of one of the publisher's salespeople, printers, or even an internal accountant, you are ahead of the game. Use that name to help you find someone closer to the editorial department.

And what with all the mergers in publishing these days don't be afraid to contact folks on the business side of a media company—for example, Time-Warner owns Warner Books and AOL (among lots of other things). If you have an "in" at AOL you probably can obtain the name of someone at Warner Books.

Okay, suppose playing six degrees of separation doesn't yield you Kevin Bacon, disguised as an editor. What do you do? Work a little harder.

Editors attend writers' conferences all the time. The advantage of that from your point of view is twofold:

1. The conferences are always held in a nice place—like Maui in winter—so you can get a tan at the same time you are trying to forge a relationship with an editor.

2. The editors who attend these conferences expect would-be writers to approach them. Indeed, they say it is one of the reasons they go to these things. (The fact that they bring their

---

4. If you don't like doing this sort of thing, you are not alone. I don't like to network. Heck, I don't like to talk to that many people outside of my immediate family. If you hate networking, and you don't know anyone in publishing, you have two choices: Resign yourself to the fact that you are never going to be published or get over your reluctance. There are no other options. Since my kids insist on eating, I learned to get over it. You can too.

golf clubs and tanning butter with them is of no import, they contend.)

Obviously, once you meet the editor at the conference, you can follow up. (What you should send him—assuming you were not silly enough to complete the whole book ahead of time—is the subject of Chapter 4.)

Okay, but let's assume networking has failed you, and as tempting as Maui is, you have decided to pass. What next? Go to your local bookstore and head over to the section that is the likely home for your book. Pull books similar to the one you want to write down from the shelf.

Yes, of course, what you are planning to write will be unique. But there is bound to be something that is fairly close. [**E.K.: Readers, don't feel bad about finding "competing" books; if there are no related titles, the publisher will probably assume that there is no market for *your* book.**] Go search the shelves and find it.

For example, while no one has done the definitive Clete Boyer biography, thousands of baseball biographies have been published throughout the years.[5] Go through the books and identify the handful you like. Then flip to the acknowledgments. Smart writers always pay tribute to their editors. Look who the authors thank as their editors and, voilà, you have the name of someone who might be able to do you some good.

Write to that person, and you are under way.

About this time when I am explaining the process of searching out an editor, somebody says, "All this sounds like a lot of work. Is there a directory that has all the editors' names? (There are several of them.) Can't I just use them to find someone to send my stuff to?"

You could. But I would suggest this only as a matter of last resort.

---

5. Again, you want to find something as close as possible to what you want to write. So if you want to write a baseball biography, search for baseball biographies, not sports biographies or historical biographies. If you want to do a book about entrepreneurship, look for books about start-ups and entrepreneurship, not business in general, and not even small business. You are trying to find a match as close as possible.

(And I am convinced that if you go through the process outlined in this chapter, you will never need to get to this point.)

It is not that I have anything against the directories. They are exactly what they purport to be, which is a listing of editors or agents or both. It is just that they tend to be:

○ *Outdated.* And that is true even if they are updated annually, as most of them are. A lot can change in a year. People quit, get fired, decide they want to edit poetry and not science books, move over to the business side to get away from annoying writers and agents. So, a remarkably large percentage of the information in the directories is not helpful.

○ *Vague.* Yes, a directory will tell you that Frederick G. Schmidlap is executive editor of ABC Books, a division of Random House. What it won't tell you is ABC is the place that does most of Random House's political books—so you might submit your idea to literally twenty other editors within Random House, editors correctly listed in the directories as handling political books since they have done at least one in their career (and probably didn't like the experience). And the directories won't tell you that Freddie has a passion for small, tightly focused books that contain one big idea, something that your research is likely to uncover. Yes, your history of city elections in Iowa since the days of western expansion is a political book, but it is not one that old Fred is going to have any interest in, even though he is listed as a political editor. Besides, Freddie is a bit of a lush.

○ *Remarkably Impersonal.* Because the directories tend to be outdated and vague, your initial attempts to contact these people are not going to be as helpful as one would like since you can include little to appeal to an editor's interests. (You don't know what they are.) Instead of pitching Frederick Schmidlap on the history of Iowa elections, it would be far more effective to write him something like this: "I read *Hanging Chads* by Peter Pundit, a book that you published a couple of years ago, and thought it was terrific. It was simple, direct, and insightful. In that tradition, I thought my book on Iowa elections would be right for you because . . ." That kind of letter is going to be far more effective than "I saw in the XYZ directory of editors that you do political books. I have a political book. . . ."

The second question that comes up at this point is, "Can't I get someone to do all this for me?"
The answer is yes. And that brings us to the subject of agents.

Do You Need an Agent?

Do you need to go through the process of searching out the right editor and publishing house for what you have to say? Of course not. You can have an agent do it for you.

But let's start at the beginning: Do you need an agent? Well, having one sure sounds good.

o If you have an agent, it means by definition you have something to sell. You have someone (your agent) out hawking your wares.

o You have (in theory) someone looking out for your best interests. (More on this in a minute.)

o You can casually drop phrases such as "I was talking to my agent and . . ."

So, do you need an agent?
I can give you a firm "maybe."
I have done books (most of them) that my agent persuaded somebody to buy and have sold a couple without an agent (including two that did embarrassingly well), and I am happy to argue the proposition either way.

It is not wishy-washiness on my part; it's just reality. To me it comes down to a question of return on investment (ROI). If, after you do the math, you think an agent can either make you more than she charges you in commissions—and figure the agent will get 15 percent of everything you sell—or save you money by freeing you up to do other things, then you go with the agent.

If she can't, you don't. Or if you'd rather do the work yourself, in exchange for keeping 15 percent more of what you receive, then don't hire one.

Agents 101

Employing agents falls in the good news/bad news category.

The bad news?

Most agents are adequate at best. That's sad, but true. And even the bad ones are expensive—just about all nonfiction agents now take 15 percent of *all* money generated by a book project. That means the agent would also receive 15 percent of things such as the sale of the paperback rights, magazine excerpts, audio recordings of the book, overseas sales, CD-ROMs, and so forth.

(There is no way around it. All the checks are sent to your agent— it is part of the agreement you sign, once he's agreed to represent you—and he gives you 85 percent of what he receives on your behalf a week, or two, or three after he receives it.)

The good news?

Well, on the most basic level it is this: Agents don't make any money unless you do. They are paid strictly on commission, much like a lawyer who works on contingency (although I have yet to meet an agent who likes that analogy). No money for you, no money to them. You aren't out a nickel no matter how hard the agent worked to sell what you have.

On a deeper level, there are good agents. They recognize a commercial idea when they hear you pitch it badly, and the best ones can help you shape it, some going so far as to edit your first pass at a proposal. (See Chapter 5.)

In addition, the good ones have an on-going relationship with editors—that is, they can get their telephone calls returned before you can. They have a good sense of which book would be appropriate for which publishing house. (Something we'll discuss next.) And perhaps more important, they can free you from most of the administrative headaches that come with getting a book published.

Someone has to haggle over the size of the advance and the contract, think about how the book should be marketed, and deal with the publisher when he is being wrong-headed (i.e., not printing enough books [**E.K.: Paul, that's *so* old-fashioned. We can always print *more*.**] and/or not spending enough to support what you have written).

Is that worth 15 percent? You have to decide. Let's go into some detail so you can.

The Argument for Agents: Pro

The following is a true story:

Every three or four months, I spend two consecutive days in Manhattan on what I refer to as selling trips.

During these visits I think of myself as being Willy Loman (the salesman in *Death of a Salesman*). I come with my sample case— which in my case is a legal pad filled with doodles about books I could write—and I knock on various doors trying to interest various editors in my spring or summer or fall or winter line of wares (books).[6]

In the best of all possible worlds, I leave with an order or two (for a new book).

Now, I learned a long time ago that it is easier to sell to people with whom you have an existing relationship, and so I spend about 80 percent of my time on these selling trips meeting with editors I already know.

But editors move on to other things: Some move into administration full-time, others become agents, and a few become (heaven for-

---

6. I know the analogy is not great, but I need something to keep me going as I walk through midtown Manhattan. As much as I hate networking, I hate selling even more, so picturing myself as someone trying to get by on "a shoeshine and a smile" helps a bit.

fend) writers themselves. [**E.K.: One of my fellow editors at Prentice Hall left to become a flight attendant.**] And so the number of editors I know steadily declines over time.

To make sure I always have as many potential prospects to call on as possible, I try to meet one or two new editors during each selling trip into the big city.

Now, I have a bit of a track record. And if you type "Paul B. Brown" into the search engine at Amazon.com, Barnes and Noble.com (BN.com), or even Google, you'll find a fairly long list of books I have written. Some you may even have heard of.

The reason for bringing that up is not to brag—believe me, I know no one cares—but to set up the following story.

Recently, confident that I had finally arrived in the publishing world after twenty years of writing books, I picked up the telephone and called a mid- to senior-level editor at an okay publishing house— it isn't the first name that springs to mind, but it is real and it is respected. I had never done any books for this particular house, and it seemed to me that it was (finally) starting to publish some interesting stuff. So, I figured meeting with him for a half hour or so during my next selling trip might be in order to see if there was any way of us working together.

He wasn't in, so I left a message on his voice mail saying who I was and that I'd like to buy him a cup of coffee. I stressed in my message that the visit would be purely social, and I figured it would take thirty minutes at most.

I never heard a word back. [**E.K.: Maybe you weren't his type.**]

A couple of weeks later I told my agent what happened, and fifteen minutes later I received a telephone call from the editor that began, "Paul, so sorry we have had so much trouble getting together by phone. By all means, let's have a cup of coffee. When is the next time you are going to be down this way?"

Agents can be good things.

And that is especially true if you don't have much of a book-publishing track record. It is hard to get an editor to read anything if he doesn't know you. If the editor knows the agent, however, you can bypass the problem.

In essence, many editors use the agent as (an unpaid) screening device. Publishers know that agents don't make any money unless the work sells. So if an agent is willing to invest his or her time on spec, the editor is more than likely to open the envelope containing your proposal and the agent's cover note, once he recognizes who sent the package. (That's why your agent, and not you, should always send out all communications.)

Not only can agents get telephone calls returned and letters opened, but the good ones can save you a lot of time.

Writers fall in love with their ideas. And that's great. Passion beats just about anything you can think of time after time. But not all deeply loved ideas are commercial. And while I may think a book by a 40-something writer contemplating his life at (hopefully) the half-way point ranks right up there with *Who Moved My Cheese* in terms of commercial potential, a quick thumbs down from my agent is enough to get me to ghostwrite another CEO autobiography so that I can make sure the four teenagers will be able to attend the overpriced college of their choice. My agent, like every good agent, has a terrific sense of what will sell and what won't.

> Having your agent shoot down an idea can save you a lot of time. It keeps you from pursuing something that is unlikely to be published.

And then there is the most obvious point of all: I am not great at negotiating anything. (I buy cars from my friend Carl Sewell, who happens to be a car dealer, so I don't have to haggle. The car shows up in my driveway, and he sends me a bill.) My agent negotiates every single day of his life, up to twelve hours a day; when it comes to getting the best terms from a publisher, he is going to be far better at it than I am.

Now the Bad News

The following is an old joke.

A struggling writer, let's call him John, receives a call on his cell phone while he is meeting with an editor about a book that is never going to sell.

> **JOHN'S FRIEND:** John, I don't know how to tell you this, but your agent spent all morning at your house. He made love to your wife, took all the cash that was in the house, and ran off with that old watch your father gave you just before he died.
>
> **JOHN:** (After a three-beat pause). Really? My agent came to my house?

Yes, agents don't always return telephone calls as quickly as you would like (let alone make house calls). No, they don't drop everything the moment you send them something new and read it. And yes, you do have to wonder why if you have done the bulk of a deal (came up with an idea, got an editor interested, and so forth) they should receive 15 percent.

So, the question for you is: Is your agent—or potential agent—worth the 15 percent?

The Problem May Be Not with Agents but with You

The easiest way to figure out if the agent is worth the money is to spend some time determining what it is you want her to do for you.

If you come up with all your ideas, feel comfortable cold-calling (and/or e-mailing) editors, and don't mind haggling over contractual terms, then you probably don't need an agent.

If you just need help on the contract and money issues, a lawyer might be a better way to go.[7]

It really is a question of what you want an agent to do for you. For example, in my case, coming up with ideas is easy. (My ideas may not be good, but boy do I come up with a lot of them.) But I need help with negotiating to get the biggest advance possible, and I also like the fact that my agent is well connected, so he knows which books currently under contract are in trouble. (I get a lot of "book doctoring" jobs.)

So, in my case, I am happy to pay the 15 percent, even if my agent is fond of making fun of my golf game.

If you are not happy paying the money, and/or you don't think the services justify the cost, do it yourself.

However, if you think you want an agent, you then need to find one. That part is easy. Getting him to represent you is more difficult.

Getting an Agent to Take You on As a Client

Let's reduce the issue to its lowest common denominator: As we said, agents don't make any money unless you do. (Here's how my agent tells me one of my book ideas is not very good: "I can't make any money selling this. Go find something commercial so we both can make some money.")[8]

Therefore, the only question agents truly have in deciding whether they want you as a client is: Can you help them? The only way that is going to happen is if you have an idea that they can sell.

But wait a second, I hear you cry. Isn't that the agent's job? Isn't she supposed to be bringing deals to me?

---

7. There are lawyers who specialize in publishing issues. This would be the way to go, if you choose the lawyer-only route despite the fact that your niece just passed the bar.

8. He has only two kids to put through college, but he owns three horses. I figure that is the same as having four kids.

The short answer is: Not at first. And maybe not ever. Why would an agent take a commercial idea and give it to someone she doesn't know? She wouldn't. The ball initially is in your court. You need to convince the agent, not the other way around. That raises two distinct questions:

1. How do you find an agent?

2. What must you do to get her to take you on as a client?

First question first.

Finding Agents

The easiest way to find an agent is to have a friend who already has one. It is not as strange as it sounds. It is just another way of saying network until you find someone who knows an agent.

For example, I did my first book with Geoff Smith (it was also his first book), and neither one of us had an agent as we set off to write that immortal classic: *Sweat Equity: What It Really Takes to Build America's Best Small Companies—By the Guys Who Did It.* (If you look hard enough, you can find it on remainder tables everywhere selling for $1.99.)

Geoff had been in the Army Reserves with a fellow named Kiril Sokoloff, who wrote books (*Street Smart Investing: A Price and Value Approach to Stock Market Profits; The Thinking Investor's Guide to the Stock Market*) and had an agent. So when we were thinking about writing a book that could logically follow on the heels of Tom Peters and Bob Waterman's *In Search of Excellence,* Geoff called Kiril and asked if he thought his very successful agent would be right for us. Kiril said yes, and so we called up Connie Clausen, a former Ringling Brothers and Barnum & Bailey showgirl, as we later discovered, and pled our case.

Connie, bless her heart, took us on, and suddenly, Geoff and I were in the book-writing business. (Geoff has subsequently come to his senses and has gone back to running magazines.)

All this is fine, but what should you do if networking fails? Well, let me expand on a point I made in passing in Chapter 1. I would *not* start by going through a directory such as the *Writer's Guide to Book Editors, Publishers, and Literary Agents.*

Let me quickly stress that there is nothing wrong with that directory or any of the others out there. My problem with using this kind of resource is twofold:

(a) I have the same objections that we talked about previously when we were discussing whether to use a directory to contact editors or not. (The information tends to be outdated, vague, and impersonal.)

(b) And since everyone else on the planet tends to use these directories when trying to contact an agent, they lose their effectiveness. As we discussed in Chapter 1, my agent receives 1,200 letters, telephone calls, and e-mails each year that he can trace directly back to being in the directory. Of those 1,200 contacts, he signs four new clients. Using a directory to find an agent simply isn't a good use of your time.

A far better approach is to do exactly what we talked about before when we discussed how to find an editor:

1. Pick up a book that is as similar as possible to the one you want to write.

2. See who that author thanks as her agent.

3. Contact the agent.

That way you know you are dealing with at least a semiqualified agent. He sold at least one book. And you know the agent has some interest in your topic.

The last is a point that people tend to overlook. Much like editors, agents specialize. It is rare, for example, to find an agent who does both fiction and nonfiction in equal amounts; and even within a specific category like fiction, some specialize further, dealing only with mysteries or maybe science fiction.

Once you know who to contact—be it the editor, if you are going to do it yourself, or an agent—you need to know what to send.

CHAPTER 4

Market Test: The Second-Best Answer Is No

The fact that you can do all of the following:

○ Explain your idea clearly,

○ Position it as something that will benefit potential readers (what we talked about in Chapter 2), and

○ Spell out how your book idea is destined to make the publisher rich

is swell, but it does not guarantee success (defined as getting published). And that, unfortunately, is true whether you have an agent pitch your idea or you propose it yourself.

I've learned this firsthand.

I could explain to you in the proverbial twenty-five words or less (nineteen to be precise) an idea I had for a book that would be called *Management Secrets from the Fly on the Wall*. ("Senior advisers to the best CEOs tell you how they really manage when no one is around to observe.") And I could position it in a sentence: "We learn what the best executives truly concentrate on to succeed, so we can, too."

But no one was interested.

Then (and you need to remember this was back in the late 1980s, early 1990s) I wanted to write *RoboManager,* in which I would identify the best traits of the best CEOs—maybe Roger Enrico's (PepsiCo) marketing skills, Larry Bossidy's (Honeywell) ability to get things done, and Sandy Weill's (Citigroup) deal-making ability—and create a fictional cyborg template that managers could aspire to.

Nobody cared.

And then there was my favorite, *A Mulligan on the Back Nine: A Year Inside the Ropes on the Senior Professional Golf Association Tour.* The title makes clear what the book would be about. Offering an inside peek at something a lot of aging golfers (like me) have always wondered about had to be a surefire idea. After all, what do you give your dad for Father's Day if not a book about golf?

Clearly, the best thing you can hear from an editor is "yes," as in "Yes, we'd love to publish your book." But "no" really is the second-best response. The worst? Any of the following: "Maybe." "Let us think about it." "I am not sure, let me do some checking." "It's not right for me, but let me give it to a colleague." (You get the idea.)

Those responses (if sincere) just leave you hanging. (If they are not sincere, you have gotten your "no.")

Man was I psyched about this golf idea.

I was so enthused that I almost violated the first rule of book writing and started to work on it without a guarantee that I was going to get paid (because I was so sure it would be published).

Fortunately, I came to my senses and got the nice people at *Inc.* magazine (Oct., 2001) to commission a piece about life on the Senior Golf Tour. While I was proud of the story, all the while I was constructing the following headline, deck, and lead I was thinking about how I would rework all my reporting and writing and turn it into a book.

You can get a good sense of what the book would have been like from the following snippet from the magazine piece:

Foreplay

It is surprisingly simple to get a shot at what appears to be some easy money on the Senior Golf Tour. The question of course is: Do you have game? Trust us, you don't.

By Paul B. Brown

Admit it.

After hitting a three iron within three feet of the pin or reeling off a half-dozen birdies, you've thought about it some. Maybe a lot.

You'd take a year off and play every day. Hire the sports psychologist. The nutritionist. The swing coach. And then, maybe, just maybe, you'd be ready for the U.S. Senior Golf Tour.

Now, you are realistic, even in your daydreams, so you don't picture yourself beating someone like Hale Irwin, 56. Irwin has won close to $20 million playing golf, and smoked players 35 years his junior—including Tiger Woods, Phil Michelson, and David Duval—to take the first round lead in the U.S. Open over the summer.

So, you don't have any expectations about being that good. But, you could beat the Jim Holtgrieves, Ted Goins, and John Scroeders of the world, couldn't you? After all, the Senior Tour is made up of a bunch of guys you have never heard of who are by definition over fifty and who are bogeying the same par fives as you it seems every time you catch them on TV.

How hard can it actually be? Even if you stunk, you take home a five-figure check each weekend for playing three rounds of golf on a beautiful course somewhere where you'll be pampered at every turn. You'll get a free luxury car to use during the tournament. You'll be handed new clubs and clothes. Heck, they will even pay you to play a certain brand of golf ball.

Sheesh, where do you sign up?

How could this not be a major bestseller? Well, it can't sell if it is not written. And I never turned my reporting into a book, because no one wanted to buy it. Like the idea for *Management Secrets from the Fly on the Wall* and *RoboManager,* every editor contacted said "no."

While I was disappointed, I am glad that I found out early that there was no market. Investing a lot of effort into something that nobody is ever going to read is a waste of time, no matter how terrific your idea is.

Besides, there is always another idea. Honest.

Ideas Are Not the Problem

A lot of people think that coming up with an idea is the key thing you need to do when it comes to getting a book published. In fact, they talk about it in hushed tones as THE IDEA, as if you need to come up with only one, and if you do you are destined to be Stephen King or Ken Blanchard. When you ask them what their book is about, they are secretive and evasive, worried that you will steal it or run and sell the idea to someone else.

What rubbish.

Sure, the idea is important. But ideas are cheap. You need to come up with a lot of them and then pick the right one, the best one, that you think is going to get you and a publisher excited. (I am assuming you are excited about the idea. If you aren't, don't do it. Why would you want to spend a year or more of your life working on something you don't love? And if the publisher isn't excited, the whole discussion is moot.)

So you want to generate a lot of ideas. And that thought leads to two others:

(a) Tempting though it may be, don't just focus in on the first one. Here's how my friend Kevin O'Connor—a man who thinks of ten ideas a day that can lead to new companies, such as DoubleClick, that he creates—put it to me one day: "It's like buying a new house, or looking for a new job. The first house you look at may be perfect. Or that first job offer might turn out to be ideal, but how will you ever truly know, unless you compare it to what else is out there? If you consider four or five, you will probably come up with a better choice." It's exactly the same with book ideas: Come up with lots of ideas, compare and contrast them, and pick the one you love best.

(b) If the publisher says no, you will at least have another idea (or two or three) that you can turn to and develop next.

Rejection Made Simple

How are you going to know if the idea is going make you a published author or lead to you receiving a letter that begins, "Thank you so much for your recent submission. Unfortunately . . ."?

Well, you could sit down and write the entire book and then send it out to various publishers. (We talked about how you approach publishers in Chapter 3.)

Although you could do that, remember our premise: We are trying to make the process of being published as efficient as possible. At the very least it will take months to write a book, and conceivably years, and you don't want to waste that kind of time if the answer is, "Sorry, we are not interested." So, we need a better way.

Option #2 is writing a full-blown proposal, the subject of Chapter 5. And the odds are you are going to have to do this at some point, if you get someone interested in your idea. However, I would not yet skip ahead to Chapter 5 (where I not only talk about how to write a proposal but also give you an annotated version of one that sold a

"No" is the second-best answer. "Maybe" will drive you nuts.

book so you can make sure what to include and, equally important, what to leave out).

Why not start on the proposal right away? Because, as you will see, creating a proposal is a lot of work. A typical proposal runs about 6,000 to 10,000 words, and who wants to write 6,000 to 10,000 words without a guarantee of getting paid? (Remember our motto: No man but a blockhead . . .)

So, my thought is to keep things as simple and as easy for you as possible when you are trying to gauge interest in what you have to say.

As long as you can reduce your idea to a single sentence, wrap a couple of questions around that sentence and, voilà, you have yourself a one-page query letter that you can send out to people whom you would love to be your editor.

For example:

Dear Editor:[1]

Maybe it's because I am the owner of what promises to be the world's tallest yellow lab, but I have spent a lot of time recently searching for the perfect book about how to raise a healthy, happy dog.[2]

I am not talking about a book about how I can bond with my dog; or how dogs are like people; or what we can learn from dogs; or travels with my dog. What I have been looking for is the *Dr. Spock's Baby and Child Care* guide for dogs.

It doesn't exist.

I'd like to write it. For you.

---

1. Never, never do this. Each of my letters was created as a real business letter and addressed to each of the editors I sent it to. The editor's full name, correct title, and business address were always used, even though they each got the identical letter. Doing anything less is unprofessional—and stupid. If you can't take the time and trouble to get the editor's name right, why should anyone believe that you will get the details in a book right?

   Will an editor think this way and reject out of hand your idea simply because you didn't bother to look up his or her name? Who knows? But why would you ever want to give anyone a reason to reject your idea?

2. Like everything else in life, if you can get people's attention things are much easier. Spend a lot of time on the opening sentence.

Having written more than a dozen nonfiction books, including *Customers for Life,* which has sold more than one million copies worldwide, I know what it takes to turn out a tightly focused service book.[3] And since nine-month-old "Buster" is already tall enough to rest his head on the kitchen table when he is sitting down, I am definitely motivated to help readers—and myself.

Some 36 million American households own at least one dog (according to the ASPCA), so we have a huge built-in market.

If this sounds interesting, I would love to talk to you.

Sincerely,

Paul B. Brown

I don't think the letter needs to be much longer than this. A page is more than enough space to make four key points:

1. You can present your idea in a single sentence. (Something, hopefully, you have already created.) In this case, the sentence is "I want to write the dog equivalent of *Dr. Spock's Baby and Child Care.*"

2. You can explain why you are the perfect person to write this book. (I have a dog, and I know how to write books.)

3. The publisher will make money, a lot of money, if it signs you up. (See the reference to the 36 million households above.[4])

4. The ball is now in the editor's court. He or she should contact you to get things rolling.[5]

---

3. Brag on yourself briefly. The point is to reassure the editor that giving you money to write the book would not be a mistake. Point out a fact or two or three (no more than that) about you that will make him comfortable.

4. The specific beats the general every time. So, instead of saying a lot of people own dogs, I went with a real number from a real authority.

5. Yes, of course, follow up with a phone call if you haven't heard anything in ten days or so.

If folks are not interested, all you are out is the time it took you to write the letter. If someone comes back to you with an expression of interest, you can develop the idea further.

Yet Another Small Step

If the editor says, "Sounds interesting, tell me more (in writing)," do you go to the proposal stage yet?

You could, but I would still argue against it. There is no guarantee that the proposal is going to lead to a book sale, and as you will see in Chapter 5, proposals are a lot of work. Editors are fond of saying, in response to either a telephone call or a query letter, "Gee, that sounds interesting, send me a proposal," as if these suckers write themselves. They don't.

Even if you write quickly, and have all the facts about your subject matter at your disposal, it is going to take you a solid week to create a proposal—and that is a full week when no income is coming in.

That is one reason for trying to do something shorter. (And again, if folks are interested, you can always expand whatever you write later into a full-blown proposal.)

There is another reason for trying to get away with doing less than a full-blown proposal. The less you have to write, the more quickly you can move.

For example, while the book may flow out of your twenty years of experience doing XYZ, sometimes the newspaper gives you a compelling idea on which you need to act quickly. You won't have a week—or more—to put together a proposal. Waiting gives someone else the time to get the idea to the editor first.

Let me give you an example.

During the midst of the corporate ethics meltdown of 2002, when it seemed every time you turned around you heard about another company (Enron, AOL, Qwest) or another CEO (WorldCom's Bernard Ebbers; Tyco's Dennis Kozlowski, Martha Stewart's Martha Stewart) doing something questionable or sleazy, I ran into my friend Jeffrey L. Seglin, who writes an ethics column for the *New York Times*.

In addition to being nice to animals and small children, Jeff has a master's degree in divinity from Harvard. He is, in short, a mensch. You can always count on him to do the right thing.

We began talking about the scandals, and the proverbial light-bulbs went on above our heads. Jeff knows ethics and business—he was my boss for a time at *Inc.*—and in theory I know something about leadership, business, and the law. If we teamed up, we thought, we might be able to do a book playing off the scandals. We didn't want to chronicle them—the daily press and the business magazines had that angle more than covered. But we could do a prescriptive book, something along the lines of *Business Ethics for Dummies.* We'd show leaders, and people who would like to be leaders, how to behave ethically.

With another piece of the various scandals unfolding every day, there was no time to do a full-blown proposal; we needed a response literally in a matter of days, if not hours, if we were to get to work.

Yet, we sensed we needed to do more than a one-page pitch because:

1. *There might be potentially competing books.* There was nothing in the works that was directly on point. But numerous books were going to be written about the individual corporate scandals so we needed to make clear what ours would and would not be.

2. *It was not intuitively obvious that this would* not *be an ethics book.* We knew ethics books don't sell. More important, we knew publishers know ethics books don't sell and so would not be in any hurry to sign up another one. But our worry was they would pigeon-hole what we wanted to write as an ethics book and not as the leadership book we envisaged. We needed more than a page to make sure what we wanted to write (a leadership book) was painfully clear.

3. *This needed to be done quickly.* We needed the book to be out a year from the day we started writing—remarkably fast in publishing, where nine to twelve months from the time you turn your manuscript in to your editor until it is in the stores is the norm. To show that we could deliver quickly, we needed to sketch out our idea in some detail quickly.

4. *To be blunt, we needed a lot of money to write this book.* Not only would there be the splitting of the advance and royalties, we would be forced to drop or postpone everything else we were doing to get this project done.

So, with that by way of background, Jeff and I hit the telephones and found two editors who might be willing to pony up serious money for the book we described.

And then they both said, in essence, "Let me see something on paper." Some twenty-eight hours later, this is what we sent them. As you can see, it is more than a one-page query letter, but less than a full-blown proposal.

● ●

If You Need an Ethics Policy, Something Is Terribly Wrong

BY JEFFREY L. SEGLIN AND PAUL B. BROWN

Adelphia Communications. Enron. Global Crossing. Qwest. Rite-Aid. Tyco. Worldcom.

And those are just the ones we know about for certain. Vivendi., PriceWaterhouse, ImClone (i.e., Martha Stewart), and who knows who else are on the horizon.

Is there any wonder that we* want to write a book called *If You Need an Ethics Policy, Something Is Terribly Wrong*?

Okay, the timing is right. But aren't all ethics books preachy and dull?

Yep.

But although it has ethics at its heart, we don't see this as an ethics book. This is a leadership/management book. Here's why:

○ The failure of almost all the companies listed above is a leadership issue, directly in the case of Adelphia, Enron, RiteAid, and Tyco, and indirectly everywhere else.

○ There is a growing body of research—detailed in a minute—that says ethics and profits are inseparable. The companies (and businesspeople) with the highest ethical standards tend to greatly outperform the Machiavellian wannabes.

○ We are convinced that ethical behavior can be as much a business strategy as excellent customer service or superior technology. If you can execute against established corporate values—in other words, if you can get your values and the way you do business aligned—you have a remarkably strong core competency.

Having hopefully established that this a leadership book with ethics at its core, let's take the "ethics are dull issue" head-on.

Scolds, Lectures, and the Bottom Line

One of the challenges of having a meaningful discussion about business ethics, whether it's inside the classroom or on the shop floor, is that mere mention of the topic too often conjures up unpleasant images: phalanxes of finger-wagging Naderites, getting their jollies at the expense of those trying to make an honest buck; armies of oversensitized poetry majors who'd sooner forfeit their every worldly possession than harm one scale on a snail-darter's back. And let's face it, nobody wants to be lectured—particularly by the likes of them.

But the notion that business ethics is primarily a mechanism of judgment, which always focuses on determining absolute rights and wrongs, is flawed. The real study of business ethics acknowledges that the choices we make are not black and white. Often, we're faced with a choice between two equally right—or equally wrong—options. As managers, do we, for example, enlist our employees' help with cost cutting at the first blush of an economic slowdown? Or instead, do we wait until we've developed a more thoughtful plan? Each will have its own implications. And when we work to think through what those implications are, we're practicing business ethics.

Broadly speaking, we like to think of making ethical decisions as weighing the impact of our decisions on the various constituencies those decisions will affect. That is the approach we will take here.

If that sounds remarkably similar to the way in which we're taught to make sound management decisions, that's because, frankly, it is. What makes the practice of ethical decision making in business so powerful is that it forces us to consider the effects of the actions we take.

Ah, but there's the rub.

What's all this thinking got to do with paying heed to the health of the business's bottom line? After all, as no less a light than Milton Friedman, Nobel Laureate in Economics, observed, a business's social responsibility is to its stockholders. Therefore, its objective should be to increase profits. Period.

That's tough to argue with, but consider the research of John Kotter and James Heskett, two Harvard Business School professors who studied the performance of 207 large firms over an eleven-year period. Their study—which has subsequently been confirmed by others—found that the more single-mindedly a company's leadership pays attention to the putative needs of the stockholders, the less those stockholders are likely to get in return.

Ironic, isn't it? Heskett and Kotter found the companies that paid attention to all constituencies—customers, employees, and stockholders—and took their needs into account when making management decisions and simultaneously put an emphasis on leadership from managers at all levels in the company, outperformed firms that did not have those cultural traits by a huge margin.

Of course, paying attention to how your business decisions will affect constituencies like employees and customers requires ethical decision making. To make the best choice, the one that may have a dramatic impact on your bottom line, you must think through the ethics of your actions.

Thinking it through is not enough, however. How you act based on that information is critical. If, for example, you've thought long and hard, understand the damaging effect of your actions, but then decide anyhow, "screw it, let's steal money from our customers, nuke the whales, and burn the pension plan," you've acted unethically—and, from a long-term management perspective, like a buffoon.

You've already seen the tone we plan to take, and the table of contents will give you a good idea of the sorts of topics we want to cover.

Table of Contents**

Introduction: Why Is This Book Necessary?

Section I: Leaders Lead

1. If you are going to be a leader, you must set an example

2. People spend an awful lot of time watching what the boss does, and if the boss is a crook, you can't expect people to be honest

3. People like doing business with people they can trust

4. You should behave

19. Why do you think they hold church every Sunday? The importance of reminding people of the corporate values

Section V: Perspective

20. There is a difference between the boss taking a 20 percent pay cut and the guy in the mailroom doing it: The difference between the top and the bottom

21. Why taking paperclips and pens home from work may not be such a bad thing

Section VI: Final Thoughts

22. We sum up and put everything into perspective

---

*Seglin, who holds a Master of Theological Studies Degree from The Divinity School at Harvard University, is the business ethics columnist for the Sunday *New York Times*. He is a regular contributor of commentaries to public radio's "Marketplace." He was also 2001 Ethics Fellow at the Poynter Institute for Media Studies.

Brown, who has been a reporter and editor for *Business Week, Financial World, Forbes*, and *Inc.*, is an attorney. He is the coauthor of several books on leadership including *Leading People* (Viking), *The Corporate Coach* (St. Martin's), and *Lessons from the Top* (Doubleday).

**Please note: These are *not* the actual chapter titles. We are just trying to describe what will be in each section and chapter.

• •

As you can see, we kept this to slightly more than 1,500 words—substantially shorter than the average proposal. Still, we communicated what we were trying to do.

So, did we sell the book?

Well, no.

The pitch was fine. The editors told us it provided them with everything that they needed to take it to their editorial boards for approval.

There was some haggling about deadlines and money [**E.K.: Paul B. Brown translation: "They wanted the manuscript yesterday and for virtually no money."**], and ultimately everyone decided not to pursue the idea. It seemed no matter how hard we tried, this was going to be positioned in the marketplace as an ethics book, and Jeff and I didn't want to spend a couple of years of our lives swimming against the tide.

Again, I was disappointed, but I would have been extremely frustrated and unhappy if we had spent a full week of our lives creating a proposal for the book only to see it suffer the same fate.

So, yes, the second-best answer to get is no.

But sometimes there is no way to find out whether the answer is going to be yes or no without writing a full proposal.

How do you create a proposal? That is the subject of our next chapter.

CHAPTER 5

Creating the Proposal

Like golf swings, pecan pie recipes, and little black dresses, there are all kinds of approaches to creating a proposal. Some are more elegant and elaborate than others, but every proposal is designed to do the same thing: Get a publisher to sign your book and write you a check.

And each proposal is written for the same reason. Editors are busy. They are typically expected to produce about twenty books a year. That's one every two and a half weeks. And while they are doing that, they are searching for the twenty books that they are going to publish next year. As much as I like to make fun of them—and I do—that is a pretty heavy workload.

As a result, they don't have time to read a finished manuscript to determine whether they want to publish it. That's why they don't ask to see a finished book (and yet another reason you don't want to write one before you have a contract to produce one). They'll ask to see a proposal instead.

I have done proposals all different ways, ranging from a two-page letter, outlining a sequel to a successful book, to a seventy-five-page opus filled with charts and diagrams for a highly technical book, where just about every concept had to be explained at length.

What follows, though, is the form that most of the proposals I have done have followed. They usually run thirty to forty pages. I find I need about seventeen to twenty pages to explain

Like snowflakes and belly buttons, each proposal is unique.

the basic premise of the book, and another thirteen to twenty pages to discuss marketing, the competition, and so forth. (Notice that about half the space is spent on "selling.") You should also know that this:

○ Really was a proposal for a book I wanted to help write.

○ Sold (to Random House) for a reasonable sum of money.

○ Was never written. Alison Davis, the main author, is extremely smart. She realized there was a lot more money to be made doing her day job—management consulting—than writing a book. She politely turned down the offer.

○ Is not perfect. As you will see, I have annotated the proposal extensively, pointing out why certain things are there and also what, if I had to do it over again, I would have improved. But I did not touch up the proposal itself. Warts and all, here's what was submitted. (How I would correct the warts can be found in the footnotes.)

• •

[1]What Women Want at Work[2]

How to Recruit, Develop, and Retain Smart Women by Managing Them Differently[3]

BY ALISON DAVIS WITH PAUL B. BROWN[4]

Something disturbing is going on in the carpeted castles of America's companies.[5] Nearly two decades after corporations first opened their gates to professional women, companies are

---

1. Notice what isn't here. There is no fancy cover. There is no cover sheet saying what follows is a proposal. On the proposal itself, you don't see the word *proposal*. And there is no table of contents to the proposal. (Although there needs to be a table of contents for the book you are proposing to write.)

Why isn't there a cover, cover sheet, and so forth? The idea is to get the reader/editor into the proposal as quickly as possible. If you want to add information, use a cover letter. (Although I would not object if you put your contact information—telephone number, mailing and e-mail addresses—in small type on the bottom of page 1.) The proposal needs to stand on its own. And if the editor needs the phrase "this is a proposal" to figure out what the document is, you are in a lot of trouble.

2. Titles are important. You need to capture the reader/editor's attention. Yes, there is about a one-in-three chance that the editor/publisher/marketing staff will insist on changing the title after they buy the book. But that is *after* the book is bought. You must get them to buy it first. A grabby title helps. This one, which plays off Freud's famous question, is good. It's not great. But it is good enough.

3. The problem with clever titles, and even semi-clever ones like this one, is they may not make it instantly clear what the book is about. This title is fairly direct. But it is possible for someone to not immediately "get" what we want to write about. That is a bad thing. So, if the title leaves any doubt, go with a descriptive subtitle—something that we did here. If appropriate, using the words "how to" is always good. It makes clear the book's goals and it implicitly promises that you are going to show the book buyer the way to accomplish something.

However, if you go this route, you need to deliver against the subtitle in the proposal. Otherwise the editor will be confused at best. So if you say the book will be about "how to recruit, develop, and retain smart women by managing them differently," then that's what it better be about.

4. Ten years ago, I would have said if you have a title or graduate degree—doctor, Ph.D., for example—leave it out. It would seem like braggadocio and be off-putting. However, experts are now all the rage. If you have a title, *and it is somehow germane* to what you are writing about, by all means include it. Don't

beginning to catch on to the fact that many of their smartest, most talented women aren't joining their male counterparts in advancing into the ranks of senior management. Instead, they've begun to defect at an alarming rate.[6]

Consider:

○ Only 10 percent of top jobs at the nation's largest 500 companies are held by women, according to an October 1996 report by Catalyst, the nonprofit research firm.[7] More than

---

put your M.A. [in English] here if you are writing *Woodworking Made Easy*. Just be sure to talk about it when you get to the "about the author" section of the proposal. (See page 84.) Do add "Ph.D." if you are doing a book on microbiology or counseling. Writing a law book, and you are an attorney, by all means use the J.D. or Esq. after your name. You get the idea.)

5. Two things to note here: The first sentence, like the title, is important. Like the "lead" in a newspaper piece, if you don't hook readers immediately, they may not keep reading. Second, you are setting the tone for what is to follow.

With this opening sentence Davis is trying to (a) set the scene, (b) be descriptive, and (c) by using alliteration (carpeted corporate castles), show she can write. Truth to tell, she probably didn't need me at all to create this document. She understood intuitively how a proposal should be constructed. (It is always nice to work with smart people.) You want to leave an editor with the feeling you know what you are doing. It's important to convey that impression right from the start. This opening, we were subsequently told by editors who saw the proposal, worked well for them.

6. Yes, the proposal seems slightly dated now, but remember it was created in 1996. At the time, the idea for the book, the data, and the conclusions were all cutting edge. In the interest of "not touching up the X-rays," I have not updated anything here, basically because Davis does an excellent job of marshalling facts as part of her effort to get an editor to buy a book. That's what's important here, not the fact that some of the information is now out-of-date. It wasn't at the time.

7. Relying on secondary sources is something that needs to be handled with care. In the best of all possible worlds, your book will be based on "your fifteen-year groundbreaking study" into whatever you are writing about. But most of us aren't researchers and don't have fifteen-year studies we can pull out of our hip pockets.

The problem with going in the opposite direction—and just citing newspaper and magazine articles, journals, and other books—is that readers are implicitly going to feel that you are not "adding value." "I could have written this" is going to be their conclusion if they see newspaper articles and magazine pieces and other books quoted over and over again. The trick is to combine outside research with your own experience. It's a tricky balance. Davis pulls it off.

100 of these companies have no women at all in senior management.

○ In a 1995 /Yankelovich Partners survey of 300 career women,
all but 13 percent said they had made, or were seriously con-
sidering making, a major change in their lives.[8] Almost a third
said they frequently felt depressed. More than 40 percent said
they felt trapped.[9]

○ Women are leaving large companies to start their own firms
at a frantic pace. In fact, companies founded by and run by
women now employ about three-quarters as many workers as
the 500.[10]

---

8. Notice by this point you are saying to yourself, "Golly, this person has done
a heck of a lot of research on this." The credibility of her argument has been
established, giving the editor another reason to keep reading.

9. If I had to do it over again, I would have put in a pithy quote from a real
woman—i.e., someone who brings to life what we have talked about so far—
right here. As you will see on page 67, for example there are quotes from
unidentified people who all say, in essence, "Yes, everything you have read up
until now is exactly right."

Those quotes are bland and generic, I now realize in retrospect. A compelling
quote—showing that this is more than a glib theoretical exercise—should have
gone here to hammer home the points that have been made so far and to show
that a lot of research had been done.

10. I'll let you in on a secret that television producers have been using for
years, and one that I borrowed in creating this proposal, and, in fact, use in all
of my proposals.

The average half-hour sitcom runs about 22.5 to 23 minutes without commercials. When they shoot the pilot—the sample show that is supposed to
convince the network that what they are being offered is the next *Friends*—
television producers deliberately have the show run up to 90 seconds short.
Pilots are anywhere from 21 to 22 minutes long, at the most. The idea is to
make network executives think that the show moved faster than it did. It is
just another subtle way that the producers try to enhance the appeal of what
they are pitching.

The same can hold true in proposals. A slightly larger font—Tahoma or Arial
instead of Times Roman—slightly wider margins, and the use of bullets can

What's Going On?

Although much has been written about the glass ceiling, the difficulties of balancing work and family, and even the executive woman's midlife crisis, these are only facets of a larger problem. It is a problem that has developed because we have denied a basic truth in our quest to create a diverse, unbiased workplace. That truth is as striking as it is basic: Men and women are different. Since they are different, we must deal with those differences in order to create an effective work environment.

If executives and managers—both male and female—are serious about recruiting, developing, and maintaining smart women, they must begin with this fundamental premise: **Women need to be managed differently than men.**[11]

At first glance, this seems like a big setback for all the gains women have made in corporations over the last three decades. After all, wasn't the idea supposed to be that women were men's equals, not constrained by biology or babies?

Women certainly have worked hard to prove that they're just as tough as men, in every venue from the construction site to the

---

make the proposal really feel as if it is moving right along, as editors read it. (You will notice all three "tricks" here.)

Smaller fonts, single spacing, and packing words densely on the page have exactly the opposite effect. That might be the way to go if you are pitching a scientific or technical book.

11. Again, you want to make the proposal interesting, and making it interesting visually is one way to do just that. Not only does using boldface **sparingly** get the information to "pop," it is also, obviously, an effective way to underscore key information. A rule of thumb? Don't use boldface more than twice in a proposal. (The more you use it, the less effective it is.) We used it only once in this one. Similarly we used all the other "packaging elements" just one time as well. You don't want editors to think you are all flash and no substance.

State Department. But despite this machisma, an increasing number of women are looking up from their desks at companies large and small and saying: "I hate this!"[12]

That's because companies run the old way—with values and rules that combine the most brutal aspects of the hunting tribe, the military, and the football team—are for women alien, dangerous, and exhausting places.

Listen to the way that women who have left particularly male companies like law firms and brokerage houses describe the place they're running from:

"It was very much a guy thing. I had to play by their rules or I was out of their game."

"If you couldn't get off on the thrill of the chase, there was no fulfillment here."

"The only times I got a pat on the back were when I screamed the loudest."

"Balance? You've got to be kidding! The biggest rewards went to monomaniacs, who worked twenty hours a day."

Seem extreme? It's not. In fact, the only difference between the kinds of companies these women are talking about and most American corporations is that the rules are more transparent in more aggressive industries. Genteel companies know how to sugarcoat and obfuscate behind gender-sensitive and conflict-

---

12. Yes, this is a serious book. But "serious" doesn't mean that the writing needs to be deadly dull and boring. If every once in a while—say every five pages to ten pages or so—you can come up with an interesting turn of phrase or maybe an entertaining aside, do it. No one likes to be bored.

Evidence to the contrary, editors are people too. They don't want to be bored and they do appreciate wit. [**E.K.: We certainly do. Keep trying.**] But, again, unless you are writing a humor book, don't go nuts with the jokes. You don't want to distract from what you are trying to say.

avoiding language and policies—policies that don't change the fact that these companies are female-unfriendly places.

How Women Are Different[13]

Why do companies seem more unfriendly to women than they do to men? The answer gets back to the premise: Women are different from men. And the difference is more important than any superficial Mars vs. Venus debate—women bring a philosophy and set of expectations to the workplace that are radically different from those held by men.[14]

The reason for this is historical. Until relatively recently, most women never served in the military. Most never played competitive sports. Very few were elected to or were appointed to government. And the majority never rose in the ranks of corporations, which are, after all, modeled on the military, sports teams, and

---

13. Editors skim, especially book proposals. Make it easy for them to always know what is going on in your proposal. Use subheads like the one on this page to both break up the text and provide a roadmap. As for subheads, clarity here is much more important than cleverness.

14. In writing the proposal, you want to anticipate questions that the editor/reader may have. Editors are going to be worried about competitors—either books that are already out there or books that will be published in the near future. Yes, as you can see on page 87, we will be addressing the competition directly in a separate section of the proposal, but it doesn't hurt to acknowledge up front that you understand your need to differentiate what you are proposing from what has come before. (Not only does it anticipate the question that is tugging at the back of the editor's mind but taking the question head on, as opposed to postponing your answer—or worse ducking it altogether—shows that you have a commercial sense and shows the editor you are as interested in selling books as the editor is.)

That is why the reference to John Gray's *Men Are from Mars, Women Are from Venus* works well here—as does the fact that the author is vaguely dismissive of the book. It shows she is aware of the competition but is convinced that what she has is either different, substantially better, or both.

The moral: The more evidence you can give to a publisher that what you are proposing will sell, the more likely it is that they are going to buy.

government in the way they are run, and the way they manage people.

As a result, women's views of the ideal way to do things came from a different part of society than men's: the home, the extended family, the club, and the community.

In this world, the values were clear. The work women did (first priority: raising a family) was important. There was time and opportunity to do that work and all the tasks that surrounded it. Women were honored for their contributions, not necessarily financially, but with recognition and respect. They could grow and develop as their families grew. Not only could they develop relationships, they were in charge of relationships with both families and friends. Since their world consisted mostly of people they knew, women could express emotions. And since work and family were the same, there was no problem balancing the two.

Anyone who has even a passing familiarity with the feminist movement knows that this world was not nirvana: Many women felt frustrated and unfulfilled. But the fact remains that this experience had a major and lasting impact, not only on the women who raised families in the 1950s and 1960s, but also on the daughters they raised.

As those daughters entered the workforce in the 1970s and 1980s, the companies they joined at first seemed like congenial enough places. After all, these women were young, unencumbered, and energetic, and the whole world seemed to be open to them. If management was remote and unsympathetic, it hardly mattered—management was made up of a bunch of old white guys, and women in junior jobs hardly had to deal with them.

But as the years went by, and women rose in the ranks, factors that had once been vague sources of discontent suddenly started to clang like fire bells. Most of the work women were being asked to do seemed meaningless, and they were asked to do it without enough time to do it well. Recognition was hard-won. Personal growth often seemed impossible. Relationships were tolerated, but not encouraged. Emotions were frowned upon; women learned that they were supposed to leave their true selves home. And balancing work and a personal life was at best difficult, and at worst heartbreaking.

The result is that women are waking up to the fact that the companies they work for aren't working for them. And they're starting to realize that they want to work in companies that are healthier, more balanced, and more sustaining than the ones men have been able to create.

Why Women Matter[15]

The fact that women are unhappy in corporations would not be a problem if companies didn't care about recruiting, developing, and retaining women. Unfortunately for companies, they have to, because:

○ A majority of buying decisions are made by women—not only in groceries and apparel but in seemingly male domains like hardware and automotive, where, for example, women account for 57 percent of all purchases. As a result, companies are increasingly realizing that they need women on board to help

---

15. Just like the early reference to *Venus and Mars*, which alluded to the potential size of the audience, this subhead tells the editor/reader up front that you know how the game is played—i.e., that you want your book to appeal to as large an audience as possible.

Yes, you will be talking about this later in your proposal, but it doesn't hurt to nod toward it in the first few pages. Publishing is a business. Editors want to sell as many copies as possible. That is not a bad goal for you to share. Writing "why women matter" is far from subtle, but then again, you aren't trying to be subtle. You are trying to sell a book.

make decisions about product attributes, packaging, and marketing that will appeal to other women.[16]

○ It's getting harder and more expensive to recruit and keep top performers, and women comprise at least half of this desirable employee segment. In fact, a recent Foundation for Future Leadership study showed that women are particularly skilled at a highly desirable attribute: effectiveness in managing others. What company wants to lose their best employees or their best managers?

○ Speaking of recruiting, top employment candidates in Generation X and Y—the under 30 crowd—are much more likely to choose a company based on culture and values than those a generation older.[17] If a twenty-eight-year-old woman perceives that a company has an unfavorable climate for women, she won't take a job at that company. This sensitivity is even more acute among in-demand recruits, such as MBA graduates. A study of 1,792 MBA students at twenty top business schools by the consulting firm Universum showed that "soft issues" like culture, people, and work/life issues played a major role in choosing where they go to work.

○ Investors may be starting to care about "people factors." An Ernst & Young's Center for Business Innovation study of 275 portfolio managers conducted by the Gallup Organization showed that

---

16. Again, timing is everything. If this proposal were written today, there would have been a reference or two to Home Depot, Lowe's, and Ace Hardware all featuring women in their advertisements—as both employees and customers. They started moving toward that shortly after the book was sold.

17. This is just a variation on a note we made earlier.

Not only has Davis pointed out—subtly—that *all* women are potential buyers of this book, she is now highlighting for the editor/reader that a subsection of that group, younger women, are likely to be substantial purchasers. This on top of the fact that managers of both genders are going to have to buy the book, in order to find out what it is that their female employees want at work, is an extremely effective approach to underscoring the fact that publishers can make a lot of money if they bring her book to market.

investor decisions are 35 percent driven by nonfinancial factors. One people issue, a company's "ability to attract and retain" talented employees, ranked fifth among thirty-nine factors investors use to pick stocks, right behind strategy execution, management credibility, quality of strategy, and innovativeness. If a company's stock price is affected by attrition of women workers, management may start to pay attention.

○ Then there's the tricky issue of corporate image and reputation. In their heart of hearts, top executives at Walt Disney, Whirlpool, and Exxon may not care that they don't have any women in top jobs. But it's embarrassing—and potentially damaging—when Catalyst proclaims this fact in the national media. How socially responsible and forward-thinking does a company look when it can't even develop and promote women (much less real minorities)?

What Companies Think Women Want

Smart companies now realize that they are going to have to do something in order to keep their high-potential women. The most common response has been to address what is still considered to be a "woman's issue": the work/family balancing act.

The media is full of success stories about companies large and small that have created a variety of programs designed to take the pressure off people juggling kids and career. And there's plenty of evidence that these programs work: Companies like First Tennessee National Corp. and Hoechst Celanese have statistics to prove that well-executed work/family initiatives lower stress, increase job satisfaction, improve retention—and even have a positive impact on customer service scores.

However, lest any company deludes itself into thinking that establishing a work/family program solves the "women problem," there are two factors to keep in mind. First, there is often a great divide between family-friendliness in theory and in practice. In a

Business Week/Boston University survey of 7,776 employees at 37 companies with established work-family programs, 60 percent reported that management didn't or only "somewhat" did take people into account when making decisions. And two-fifths said work had a negative impact on their home lives. In other words, even the most well-intentioned program may not be helping if it's not being supported by managers.

That ties into the second, more disturbing point: At many companies, taking advantage of such programs is a career kiss of death. To be successful in a lot of companies, a woman has to conform to the image of someone who doesn't have an outside life, who doesn't have a family, and who doesn't have any interests outside of work.

Smart women get the message: In order to succeed, they must act like men.

My Life As a Man[18]

I first realized that success meant acting like a man at my first real job, at a large public relations agency in Manhattan. This was a civilized place that employed nice people who all attempted to treat even the most junior underling (me) quite well. As a matter of fact, after I had been on the job about a month, some of the male account executives went out of their way to invite me to join the softball team. Klutz that I was, I declined; but I later realized that I was being paid the highest compliment by being included in the most important guy experience in the company.

---

18. At some point, you have to explain why you are the perfect person to write the book you are proposing. That's especially true if you are not doing original research, or basing what you are writing on "a groundbreaking study." You can make the case for why you are the perfect person to do this in the author section (see page 84), in the first part of the proposal, or conceivably both, if you can do it without being redundant.

You be the judge of whether Davis has made a convincing case in this section.

Either you were involved in softball (cheering on was okay, but not as good as being on the team) or you weren't in the game. No wonder my (female) boss who hated sports felt so frustrated and excluded!

This fairly benign example of guy-dom did not prepare me for my next job, where I worked for two women bosses. The company was run by a man who was a genius at public relations, but who was also petty, paranoid, and mercurial. My two bosses, who were both vice presidents, handled the top guy's moods in different ways.

The first woman took the heat herself, then waited until the storm had passed before calling in her staff to discuss the action required.

But my second boss was determined to be as tough as the boss—as tough as a man. Somewhere along the way in her career, she had concluded that success in business looked something like boot camp, and she had to play the role of drill sergeant. If the general was unhappy with the condition of the camp, then she had to line up the recruits and give 'em hell! Being smart and proud and in my twenties, I was determined to take this abuse like a man. Hell, I could do the seventy-five push-ups required! I could work all night on a report that really wasn't due the next morning, but the sergeant had screamed that we'd better get it done early! I could swim and march and take the punishment!

I could do all that, but I could also feel miserable. And, in what was a big surprise to me, the more I succeeded, the more miserable I felt. I'd go home every night and lie on the bed, too exhausted by the day's ordeal to do anything but stare at the ceiling. Even a promotion and a big raise didn't seem to make a difference. If I was so tough—and successful—what the heck was wrong with me?

What One Woman Wanted

I'd like to say that I woke up one morning and saw the light and realized that the problem wasn't with me but with the way I was being managed. But like many realizations, this one dawned slowly and took many years to become fully illuminated.

What happened was this: After a couple more jobs, I decided that I wasn't well-suited to working in companies, and I began freelancing. Soon, thereafter, I was sick of working at home; I hated the isolation, the lack of structure, and the feeling that what I was doing wasn't "real work." Around this time, I met a woman named Betsy who was also freelancing, and who was also sick of it.

We liked each other, and we had complementary skills, in copywriting, in public relations, and in a new area called employee communication. Maybe we should get together, we said. Rent an office together, we said. Maybe even go into business, we said.

And so, in 1984, we did. But being who we were, we didn't just call the lawyers and have them draw up the papers. We talked for months about what we wanted to do, and how we wanted to do it. We recalled what we'd hated about companies we'd worked for in the past. We spoke about the importance of having a balance between work and the rest of our lives, about how essential it was to have good relationships at work, and about how we wanted to treat each other and the people who someday would work for us.

Even in those early stages, it seemed that the company we were creating was unlike any other company we'd ever experienced. Nobody we knew was talking about the quality of life as it pertained to work, and, although we didn't have a clue about how to accomplish this lofty goal, it certainly seemed right to us. It is what we wanted from work.

A New Way of Working

So we began. Our first brochure trumpeted our philosophy along with our talents, and more than one potential client told us they were struck by the uniqueness and good sense of our approach.

As Betsy and I continued to grow our consulting business, I kept encountering women who were amazed and intrigued about our company's commitment to working differently. The most dramatic reaction came from the women we hired, many of whom were shell-shocked after working in dysfunctional companies of all sizes run by people of all genders.

Although the key dysfunction at those companies was lack of understanding that employees might have a life outside the office, there was another, more insidious problem—a problem refugees summed up as "insensitivity."

"I worked so hard at that project and my boss never expressed the slightest bit of appreciation," said one woman.

"I didn't even realize how anxious I was all the time until I came to work here," said another.

"One day at my old job I was so upset that I burst into tears. Later, my boss told me that was 'unprofessional,'" recalled a third.

So we went along, trying to create a new work environment until 1995, when we found ourselves struggling with a strange problem: Too much business was making it difficult for us to honor our value of giving people a balance between work and their personal lives. When the year started, I had had a personal goal of spending more time with my kids, and I was failing miserably. Like me, others in our then fifteen-person company were working too many hours, facing too many deadlines, and feeling too stressed-out.

Aware of the problem, but not sure we could do anything about it in the short term, we decided to convene a special staff meeting. We talked about our values, and about the importance of balance, and discussed some ways of shifting projects to take some of the pressure off.

"The thing is, it's not like we want to turn down any of these projects," said one staff member. "I mean, it's such interesting and challenging work, and it's really what we want to do."

Another person concurred. "Absolutely. It's just that there's too much of it."

"I just don't want to see any of us burn out or feel alone in this," I said. I had been struggling for weeks to define the value that we were trying to achieve during this stressful time, so I kept talking: "I want this to be the kind of company that's intellectually challenging, but emotionally safe."

One of our employees, a young woman, spoke. "Intellectually challenging, but emotionally safe," she said. "That's what I've always wanted at work."

What Women Really Want

Our company is hardly perfect, but we have gotten one thing right: By pursuing our own value of creating a company where balance and feelings are recognized and pursued, we've built a better work environment. It's a better environment for men and women, of course, but it has special resonance for the women who have felt so out of place in other companies.

So the moral of the story is that, in order to retain great women workers, companies must do more than address work/family issues—they must fundamentally change the way they manage women.

What do women really want at work? Based on my own experiences, and that of hundreds of clients, business associates, and employees we've spoken to over the years, it's clear that there are seven key factors:[19]

1. *A job where they can make a difference, where what they do matters.* Women want to feel that their work is important—at the very least to the success of the company they work for. That's one of the reasons women with career options are likely to leave a job that they perceive is meaningless and go work for an organization where they can make a contribution—to the company, to their field, to the community, or to society—even if making such a change requires a pay cut.

2. *The ability to do a good job, to succeed at the craft of work.* It's politically incorrect to say, but women care more than men do about getting tasks done—even something as mundane as making sure all the *t*'s are crossed and the *i*'s are dotted. Yet increasingly companies treat the essential basics as if they're afterthoughts, neither allowing sufficient time for them nor giving credit for managing them well. Craft matters to women, and they need to know it matters to their employers as well.

---

19. You need a hook. If you think about the book proposal as being a business plan—which it really is—then what we have talked about up until this point in the proposal has been strategy, the overarching approach the book will take. Here, we get into a discussion of tactics—how the book will accomplish all the things we have talked about so far.

Editors (and readers) like it if you discuss your tactics (i.e., the approach you plan to take in writing the book) for three reasons:

First, it shows them that you are indeed going to do all the things you promised.

Second, it gives them a good idea of how the book will lay out. It provides them with a roadmap, if you will.

Third, it gives the publisher's marketing department some ideas they can use in promoting the book.

And so, Davis provides them with "the seven key steps to making sure women get what they want at work." It may be a bit hokey to present the material this way, but it is effective. (That is why so many nonfiction books have "the six principles" or the "four-step plan to . . ." and the like.)

3. *Recognition for their accomplishments.* Talk to women in a typical (read: male-dominated) company, and you'll find out how frustrated they are about having to fight for recognition. Women don't have the sharp elbows and blocking-and-tackling training of men, and they don't feel comfortable always having to ask for praise. "Can't somebody just say 'thank you,' without me having to demand appreciation?" say women in corporations everywhere. "I need to be recognized, but if I have to beg, it's just not worth it."

4. *A chance to keep learning and growing.* Women—especially those of the baby boom generation and younger—have the expectation that they will continue to learn and grow all their lives. Even if the job doesn't change, they feel that the challenges should increase. That's why they're surprised to find themselves in organizations that value the status quo instead of celebrating development. No wonder they feel stymied and stifled.

5. *A place to form and build relationships.* It should come as no surprise that women—who have traditionally been the social force within families—value relationships. What companies aren't prepared for, however, is the fact that women want something from organizations that is no longer considered mandatory: a social network that creates its own family feeling. Although conventional corporate wisdom over the past few years has been that that expectation is unrealistic and that all that matters is profitability, recent thinking about teamwork and productivity may indicate that women have been right all along: It's relationships that matter.

6. *A safe haven, where emotions can be expressed without penalty.* The corporate soul guru David Whyte talks about how ridiculous it is for corporations to believe that employees can leave their emotions at home when they come to work. Women in companies have long felt uncomfortable with the overt prohibition that companies place on expressing emotions in the office. They feel that feelings should be allowed, and that laughing, getting angry, or crying shouldn't be career-ending episodes.

7. *Balance between work and the rest of their lives.* Yes, it's true: Women would like to have a job and a life, too. And they'd like their companies to adopt work-family policies that don't penalize people who use them. Wouldn't it be wonderful to think you could work reasonable hours and still be valued enough to be promoted—maybe even become CEO someday?

How the Book Will Be Structured[20]

We see the book having two interrelated elements. First, of course, are the seven things that women want at work. Each of the seven items will get its own chapter where we:

○ Talk about the problem. (For example, why is it that women don't get a chance to succeed at the craft at work?)

○ Explore alternatives that both women and the companies they worked for tried in an effort to fix the problem and show what did not work and why. And then,

○ Present a solution in detail and have the employees and their managers explain what the benefit was.

> These seven chapters, one for each principle, make up a key component of the book, so much so that within the chapter there will be "callouts," such as this one, to underscore major points.[21]

---

20. Don't assume that editors will know how you are going to present the material, based on the proposal. Don't leave anything to chance. Tell them directly how the material will lay out and then show them.

21. Remember, one of the things the proposal is supposed to do is show the editor/reader how you plan on presenting the material. If you are going to use things like callouts (a different kind of text design intended to break up the page; here we threw a box around the callout to make it stand out even more) in the book, use callouts in your proposal. The less an editor has to imagine, the happier she is going to be.

Wherever possible show *and* tell what you plan to do.

In addition, each of these seven chapters will end with a "Things to Do Monday Morning" checklist that will allow the reader to immediately put into practice what he or she has learned.

But while these seven chapters are extremely important, they don't represent the entire book. For one thing, the problem-solution-benefit model is the way men think. For another, it shortchanges the description of what is really happening as women, and the organizations that employ them, struggle to create a better workplace. The transformation is not linear, and indeed as you change one part of the way work is done, you invariably alter—sometimes for better, sometimes for worse—other parts of the process.

Since that is the case, *What Women Want* [22] will contain a second, equally important component. Between each of the seven core chapters will be far shorter chapters—some that will be only a page long. We have come to think of these inserts as Snapshots from the Evolution.

While the seven primary chapters will certainly contain quotes and descriptions, these snapshots will go further. They will be anecdotal, and you will hear at length—and with surprising candor—from people who are wrestling with issues that develop with changing the way we work. [23]

For example, three women will describe the conversations they had during a weekend canoe trip, and how being sucked into an unexpected rapid convinced them to go into business together. The (male) manager at MCI, who is revered by every woman in his department, will talk about how he came to the conclusion that "women are different, and that is a good

---

22. I like using my title for the book in the proposal. By doing so, it is my fond hope that the editor/reader will become smitten by it the more he hears it. And a smitten editor is one whose publisher is more likely to write a check.

23. Again, hindsight being 20–20, I might have put in an example showing how this would work.

thing," and as a result started managing differently the women in his department.

The purpose of these inserts is to give a more complete feel to the change process.

How People Read

Much as authors would like to believe the contrary, it is our experience that people do not read business books linearly. We understand that some people will be interested in only the core chapters, while others will spend most of their time on the so-called softer stuff, the stories that make up the inserts.

Either approach is fine with us, although we feel reading both elements will give a fuller, richer picture of what women truly want at work.

And it is exactly because we want to present a complete picture that we selected the companies we have—they will range from start-ups to some of the biggest companies in the world.[24]

That only seems fair. Retaining good employees is not an issue limited to only the Fortune 500. It is of deep concern to small, entrepreneurial companies as well. Companies of every size, located throughout North America, will be profiled here.

The choice of some of those companies won't be surprising. Indeed, when it comes to creating an environment where women feel comfortable, they can be called the "usual suspects." So, you will, indeed, find Catalyst award winners such as Knight-Ridder, McDonald's, and Deloitte & Touche represented here. And you will also see some overlap in our corporate lineup with "The Best 100 Companies to Work For." You'll be hearing

---

24. Yet another chance to show the potential breadth of the audience. You don't have to hit people over the head, but do what it takes to get the point across. Remember what a proposal is at heart—a marketing document. If you have a chance to sell (subtly) what you have, take it.

from people who work for companies such as Mary Kay Cosmetics and Federal Express.

But while the selection of these companies—and they probably will represent only about a quarter of the corporations mentioned—is not surprising, how we will be using those usual suspects might be. Not every one of these companies is doing everything correctly. And while it is certainly helpful to profile what they are doing right, it is equally constructive to point out where they are struggling.

Indeed, what the "best" companies are going through is really no different from the challenges facing the other companies in this book. That's why we are including relatively unknown companies—both big and small. And it is also why the book will rely as heavily as it does on the people to be profiled, within both the inserts and the core chapters. This is, after all, their story.[25]

---

25. If I had to do it all over again, I probably would have tried to come up with some kind of boffo ending for the first part of the proposal. This one kind of tails off. There should have been an overt signal of some kind saying it is time to move on to the next part of the proposal.

About the Authors[26]

Alison Davis is president of Davis•Hays & Company, a consulting firm based in Bergen County, N.J., that specializes in helping companies implement organizational change. Her firm works with such Fortune 500 companies as Aetna, Citibank, Johnson & Johnson, and Texaco to design programs that cascade corporate strategy throughout the organization and effect culture change. *What Women Want at Work* flows directly out of her research and client work over the last fifteen years.

A sought-after corporate speaker, Davis is president of CCM, the Council of Communication Management, a national organization composed of Fortune 500 executives and top consultants.[27]

A former writer and editor for *Forbes, Business Week,* and *Inc.,* Paul B. Brown is the coauthor of *Leading People,* just published in paperback by Viking/Penguin, and of the international bestseller *Customers for Life* (Doubleday/Currency), which has sold more than 800,000 copies to date. As a former manager of a fifty-person department, he has grappled firsthand with the issues raised in *What Women Want at Work*.[28]

---

26. One of the things you want to do is start different parts of the proposal—the about the author, marketing, and competition sections—on different pages. It looks better, and it makes the proposal easier to follow. (And as we talked about earlier, when we were mentioning tricks of the trade, it makes the proposal seem to move along at a faster pace.)

27. This needed to be stronger. Davis was head of a then fifteen-person management consulting firm. Her bio is weak. She isn't. I missed a major opportunity here. Make sure you don't. Put the author (you) in the absolutely best possible light. Editors like their authors to be authorities on their subjects. Davis is, and I did not get that across here.

28. Publishers frequently get nervous about first-time authors. They aren't convinced they can write a book. If you are teaming up with someone to help you, even if all they are going to do is help, put their bio in the author section. It will make the publisher feel better, especially if your collaborator has previously done a book.

Who Will Read This Book?[29]

We thought long and hard about how to say this, and in the end decided to be blunt: *What Women Want at Work* is being written for every single person in the workplace.

This is not only a "women's book." As the subtitle makes clear, this is about "how to recruit, develop, and retain smart women by managing them differently." That is an issue that is of great concern to all managers—male and female—as well as to women in the workforce.

So, the first point to stress is that *What Women Want at Work* will appeal to all managers working in companies of any size. For managers, *What Women Want at Work* will provide a practical guide on how to truly manage women differently, in a way that will make women more productive, more satisfied, and more likely to stay with the company. Of course, like any "how to change" or "how to manage" book, the ideas and suggestions in *What Women Want at Work* won't work if they're applied superficially or maliciously. Like smart workers everywhere, women won't be manipulated by slogans and the appearance of change; only real and significant change will make a difference in the way they feel about their jobs.

---

29. You need to give publishers all the help you can when it comes to positioning your book. They put out a lot of books each year and, to be candid, they are not the world's greatest marketers.

There is a tendency to short-shrift the marketing section of the proposal. That is a big mistake. You want to explain in no uncertain detail how you think they should sell your book. **[E.K.: See note 31.]** The more work you do, the less the publisher will have to, which will make them happy. And if you explain how you think the marketing should work, you have a better chance of getting what you want when it comes to promoting the book.

If you wait for the publisher to take the initiative when it comes to marketing, you are bound to be disappointed.

The second idea we would like to get across is that this book will be a resource for corporations large and small. In particular, large corporations are, indeed, finally noticing that their best women are leaving. They want to know what to do about it. However, every company wants to know how to retain the best employees, and *What Women Want at Work* will serve as a valuable resource.

The last point to make about the audience is perhaps the most obvious. This book will find a huge readership among women in the workplace. It will show them they are not alone. It will also provide them with a detailed roadmap—one in large part created by their peers—that shows how to improve (or escape from) an unpleasant work environment.

About the Competition

There really isn't any.[30]

Up until now there have been three types of books that have looked at women in the workforce. The first is of the school that says women make better managers. While intriguing, things such as *The Female Advantage* and *The Women's Ways of Leadership* don't really appeal to a wide audience and are not particularly helpful to managers—male or female—who are trying to do their jobs more effectively.

The second type, and there are scores of them, is geared solely for women and is aimed at helping them to achieve balance in their lives. It is a worthy goal, and one that we believe in, but it is only a minor focus of what we are trying to do here. Indeed, we believe women will achieve balance as a natural outcome of creating, or working within, companies that follow the principles described in *What Women Want at Work*.

The last alternative, represented most recently by such books as *How to Succeed in Business Without a Penis* and *The Princessa: Machiavelli for Women,* in essence tell women how to prosper in a man's world.

---

30. In all the years I have been creating proposals, this may be simply the worst sentence I have ever written. **[E.K.: I'll second that.]**

Every book has competition. You can make fun of the competition, dismiss it out of hand, or say only an idiot would buy what competitors have out there (and explain why) but PLEASE don't say your book is unique. It ain't. And I don't care what you are writing. There is competition for it in some form—and as you can see from the rest of the discussion in this section, we acknowledge that fact about *What Women Want at Work*.

We should have done it up front. I goofed. Big time. I have learned from my mistake. I no longer say "we don't have any competition," and you shouldn't start to say it.

They are both clever and well reasoned. But:

(a)   Most women are not comfortable taking on masculine traits, for whatever reason.

(b)   These books are geared solely to women.

(c)   These types of books do nothing to alter the male-dominated corporate landscape.

Instead of trying to push the existing mold—by showing women how to act like men—why not break the mold and create a better workplace? That's our objective.

A Matter of Perspective

There is another important point to make in talking about the competition. Up until now every book about women in the workplace has been written from one perspective, that of the woman worker. (You, gentle reader, are a female manager; here is what you should do.) Most books are written for someone fairly low down the corporate pyramid who is staring up at a hostile company and wondering how to use machete and guts to survive in that jungle.

What Women Want at Work will contain all points of view. We will talk to managers (both male and female) as well as women being managed. That way, we will provide our readers with perspectives from all angles of the problem, so that we can best help all our readers solve the challenge of how to give women what they want at work.

How the Book Will Be Marketed

We believe *What Women Want at Work* will be a marketer's dream. The point of view of *What Women Want* will make it both topical and controversial—this will not be a book that will be universally loved but will be debated over and talked about. The subject of women in the workforce has become a hot topic in both the business press and the general media, and this book will ignite the argument.

Our very premise—*Women need to be managed differently from men*—is bound to trigger huge amounts of publicity, attention, and interest. It is an easy hook for the daytime talk shows, as well as for the Sunday magazines and newspaper feature writers. In fact, it is hard to imagine a media outlet where *What Women Want at Work* would not be appropriate. It is certainly right for the morning television shows (*Today, CBS This Morning,* etc.) You can easily see Oprah doing a show—and even making *What Women Want* one of her "book club" selections—and it is difficult to imagine a women's magazine that wouldn't find the topic intriguing.[31] The idea fits in with most talk radio formats as well.

There are other benefits. The fact that we will be including so many companies as examples opens up special sales opportunities, and we expect the people we interview to be willing to cooperate in promoting the book, whether it be agreeing to do interviews with their local media or appearing on national talk shows as part of a panel.

---

31. A snotty agent I know—not mine—refers to this as the "PFO" clause, as in Perfect for Oprah, and contends every proposal now has this clause. He may be right, today, but I know for a fact he wasn't when we created the proposal. [E.K.: **Authors sometimes have blind spots about this. So before you include the PFO clause in your proposal on import/export management, please ask five people who aren't afraid to tell you the truth whether *they* think the book is PFO.**]

Even if you think readers/editors are going to dismiss it as just so much puffery, include every marketing venue you can think of. In the words of Jewish grandmothers everywhere, "it couldn't hurt," and the broader you can make the appeal of what you are selling, the better the chance you have of selling it. Don't lie and don't be ridiculous in your claims. *Regis and Kelly Live* are not going to have you on to promote your book on quarks. But, this book really could have been perfect for Oprah.

Obviously, Alison Davis should take the lead in promoting this book. She has been interviewed on television and for print countless times and is a recognized authority in her field.

In addition, her coauthor, Paul B. Brown, has been interviewed hundreds of times, by radio, television, and newspaper reporters in conjunction with his previous seven books. As a former executive (managing editor of *Financial World* magazine; marketing editor of *Business Week*), he can certainly provide the male executive perspective on this topic.

Both Davis and Brown have extensive media contacts and are committed to doing every interview either you—or they—can arrange.[32, 33, 34, 35]

---

32. If you have a coauthor use him. Let the publisher know that you are both available to do interviews, promotion, etc. That way you can really be in two places at once—or at least your book promotion efforts can. (The "name" or main author, Davis, in this case, does the major TV interviews and the like. But you can still sell a lot of books doing morning radio in Dayton. Those are the places to put your coauthor to work.)

33. You will notice there is no sample chapter. Do you need one? Yes, almost all of the time.

The only exception occurs if you take the approach that we did here and spend twenty pages explaining the book and giving what essentially are examples from what would be the finished text. Having spent this much time on what in essence could have been excerpts from sample chapters, we decided a sample chapter wasn't needed.

You probably won't be so lucky. Plan on writing a sample chapter. Yes, it is a lot of work, but you will be able to use the chapter in the finished book.

Resign yourself to the fact that you are going to have to write a sample chapter and keep reminding yourself that since it is going to be in the finished book, you are just getting a head start on the work in front of you.

34. For exactly the same reasons there was no sample chapter, there was no table of contents in this proposal. In essence, the "seven points" discussion served as the T of C. Odds are you will need to create a table of contents to show how your book will lay out.

35. Again, hindsight being perfect, I probably would have created some kind of ending for the proposal as a whole.

As these things go, I like this proposal and would have given it a B+ or A–. It could have been stronger, but it worked, as proven by the fact that someone offered to buy the book.

CHAPTER 6

Trying to Hold on to Control

If you take a step back and think about what we have discussed so far, you will notice an interesting fact: Up until this point, you have had complete control of the process.

○ You decided whether you were going to write the book.

○ You decided on how you would approach your subject matter.

○ You decided on how you were going to try to sell what you wrote (with an agent or without; through a traditional publisher or on your own).

At each step, you and you alone determined how you would proceed.

Once you submit your proposal to a publisher, however, control shifts completely. The publisher will decide whether or not they are going to bring the book to market. If they say no, you have only one decision to make: Do you want to give up or try someone else (recognizing that "someone else" could be you through self-publishing).

But if they say yes, the journey isn't over. It is (pardon the cliché) just beginning. If you get a telephone call—and it is almost always a telephone call—from a publisher who says he wants to publish your book, my suggestion is to pour yourself the adult beverage of your choice, take a sip, and then pause for a long time before you actually sign the contract that will eventually show up in the mail.

The initial contract they send you will contain at least four significant areas where you will be giving away control in exchange for hopefully getting your book published.[1]

The publisher will dictate:

○ What they want you to write

○ How they plan on selling what you write

○ How they will pay you

○ Whether they have first dibs on your next book

Now, ultimately, none of these four areas may represent a problem, but you need to know up front what they are asking you to agree to. Let's take the potential issues one at a time and discuss in detail what your alternatives are.

Let's begin with something you probably thought would never be an issue: what they want you to write.

"You Want to Write What?"

You might think that once the publisher makes you an offer there would no discussion about the content of what you want to write. After

---

1. Why "hopefully"? Because as we will see in a minute, just because you sign the contract, it doesn't guarantee that your book will ever see the light of day.

all, you have spelled out fairly clearly what you want to do in your query letter and/or proposal, and they bought the book. So, they must have agreed with your vision, right?

Not necessarily.

The editor may have thought your ideas were close to perfect, but she may want to tweak them a bit. Or, the editor might have loved the subject matter and the way you write, but she might want to change the point of view. ("Why not write the exploration of the Northwest Passage from the viewpoint of a beaver, instead of Lewis and Clark," the editor suggests.) Or . . . and there could be 100 or more *ors,* suggestions about how you might approach the material. My favorite example is the publisher who offered a friend of mine $500,000 for a book and didn't want what he was buying. My friend had been incredibly successful the last time out, and this new publisher wanted to be known as the person who brought out the sequel. My friend laid out what would have been the logical sequel to his hit; the publisher bought it and then said, "Why don't we go in an entirely different direction?" Honest.

The point is that often editors view the proposal, the very proposal that got them to write you a check, as a starting point for a serious discussion about what a book will contain and not as a blueprint.

Is that a problem?

Not necessarily.

Some editors are smart. They might have good ideas and, who knows, maybe you'll like the idea of writing about the exploration of the Northwest Passage from the perspective of a beaver. (It is different, you have to concede.) **[E.K.: That's enough. Paul, you know full well that it was not the *beaver* I suggested, but rather the *log* (i.e., strong team player; no need for frequent meal breaks; intelligence routinely underrated).]**

But, maybe you won't care for the editor's suggestions. Or maybe you'll think the editor's ideas are flat-out wrong at best (and stupid at worst). It is best to get this hashed out up front, and preferably in writing. If your vision and the editor's are not in alignment going in, there

**Once you've sold your idea to a publisher, it can be
hard to hold on to control.**

will be trouble—perhaps serious trouble later on—and you are the one
who is bound to lose.

Here's why.

In every single book publishing contract there is a clause that is
similar to the following.

"The author agrees to deliver a finally revised manuscript . . . *satisfactory to the Publisher in form and content.*" (I added the italics,
but to be honest, I think the publisher should have put them there in
the first place and put them in boldface to boot.)

What the clause means is simple: If you and the publisher differ
over the quality of what you turned in, the publisher wins. He, not
you, determines what is satisfactory.

If the publisher is not happy with what you turn in, you are, to use
the vernacular, screwed.

Now, sometimes you can insert a clause that says the publisher
can't be arbitrary in withholding approval, and you might be able to
find other words to limit the publisher's potential action, but the fact

remains that the publisher—and only the publisher—is going to decide what is publishable and what isn't.[2]

This is not hyperbole. It is fact. You have, indeed, given up control in writing. The contract will say that the publisher must be happy; otherwise he does not have to bring out your book (and may demand his money back as well).

Now, publishers don't like to invoke this clause for a number of reasons.

First, they are in the business of publishing books. If they say no to all completed manuscripts, they have nothing to publish. You can't be a publisher if you never publish.

Second, if they use the clause too often, they won't attract authors. Where would you rather submit your manuscript, to a place known for rejecting finished books or one that is known for working with its writers?

2. What happens if the publisher says, "Sorry, we read what you wrote and we can't publish it"?

Usually a lot of screaming and yelling. [**E.K.: As I recall, you didn't actually scream; though you did hurl my Robin Ventura "Grand Slam Single" memento paperweight with a respectable amount of mustard.**]

After that, a number of things could happen. For example, you could try to amend the manuscript to correct what the publisher views as deficiencies. That is usually the easiest and most efficient thing to do; and about 85 percent of the time, you and the publisher can reach common ground.

If you don't want to, or you think the publisher is completely wrong about what she thinks needs fixing, you can try to sell your book to someone else. Whether you have to repay the advance the publisher gave you will be a matter of negotiation. Typically, if you sell the book elsewhere, your initial publisher—the one that rejected your manuscript—is going to expect to be repaid out of the money you receive from publisher number two.

But like just about everything in life, this is negotiable. It could be possible to keep both advances, which turns the first publisher's rejection into a good thing. Don't count on it happening, but it sometimes does happen.

If you can't resell the book, the publisher may ask for the return of whatever initial advance you received. Whether you have to repay it is an open question. Whenever you get the letter that says "please return our advance," it is time to hire a lawyer who specializes in publishing matters, or to turn the matter over to your agent if you have one.

Third, the decision to reject a book can cause a lot of image problems among a publisher's stakeholders.

Some background will explain why this is the case.

Publishers put their books out at regular intervals. Some have a summer list and a winter list, which governs what titles they will put out from March to August and September through February while others are governed by the seasons, a spring list, a summer list, and so forth.

No matter what the frequency, many months before the books are shipped, the publisher mails out a glossy catalog and/or a slick CD putting every book on the upcoming list in glowing terms, while holding fire-up-the-troops meetings to inspire enthusiasm among the sales force.

Once both these things happen, the publisher is seriously committed to the book. If the publisher tells the sales force, "We have this huge book for spring, the story of the exploration of the Northwest Passage as told from the perspective of a beaver," and subsequently doesn't publish the book, then:

○ The publisher loses credibility with the sales force and the booksellers, who are less likely to be enthusiastic about the publisher's next offering. (They held a space for "the beaver book" and it never showed up, and so they will have this nagging thought in the back of their minds that the publisher's next book also won't show up.)

○ When the book is actually published later, if it is published, no one is enthusiastic at all. ("This was the book, *The Beaver's Tale*, about the exploration of the Northwest Passage that we were hoping to have in the stores six months ago; who cares now?")

As a result, publishers desperately try to publish books that they have listed in their catalog.

Here's how this affects you. Even though publishers know that they have at least nine months to get a book into the stores once authors turn in their manuscripts, they never seem to be able to coordinate the catalog copy for the book and the edited manuscript. Invariably, the catalog goes to the printer well before the editor signs off on the finished manuscript.

That can lead to the situation where a publisher wants to kill a book—or at least send it back for substantial rewrites—and simply does not have the option. If the publisher demands a massive rewrite, it will miss what it told the world would be the official publication date for the book.

In these situations, publishing becomes odd and sometimes comical. (And for some reason, I always seem to be in the middle.)

For example, in the midst of the corporate ethical meltdown of 2002, a senior editor at one of the major publishing houses had a terrific idea for a book. He contacted a leading financial expert and charged him with writing about how individual investors could use the lapse in business ethics to their advantage.

To be honest, the editor didn't care what Mr. Big wrote, as long as the book would deliver against the premise that individuals could profit (indirectly) from the sleazy behavior of CEOs, financial analysts, and assorted other insiders.

Mr. Big went off to write the book on his own, and two months before the deadline he dropped off a first draft that read as if he had a couple of beers and then started dictating into a tape recorder.

At this point, I got a call. The editor wanted to know if I could help. While what Mr. Big had written was amusing, the editor said he was looking for something more substantial than the seemingly stream-of-consciousness ramblings from a market insider.

I spent some time with Mr. Big and reworked huge hunks of the manuscript.

But a funny thing happened on the way to getting the book onto the shelves of your local Barnes and Noble and listed on Amazom.com.

Perhaps because he didn't want to take another shot at it, or perhaps because he really pictured himself as a writer and not the financial whiz that he is, Mr. Big took it upon himself to revise large parts of the book—after he and I had agreed the reworked version was in pretty good shape. He then sent his version of the material, one chapter at a time, to the editor, after the editor had already signed off on the reworked version that I sent him.

His editor would get the stuff and call me saying, "Have you seen this?"

I'd say no, and the editor would send it back to me for polishing. Mr. Big would sign off on it and then three weeks later he would once again rewrite it on his own, basically taking out all of my changes (changes he had seen and agreed to twice).

This became annoying—and time consuming. So time consuming in fact that it was clear that the publisher was in real danger of not getting the book into the stores on time.

The solution? The editor took the first two-thirds of the book— the parts that Mr. Big and I had worked on together—and sent it off to the printer, and he then attached Mr. Big's reworking of the final third.

The book disappeared without a trace.

But at least it got out.

In my favorite example of what I have come to think of as the game of "rejection chicken," one of the best-known business speakers in the country delivered his manuscript to his publisher who looked at it and said, "You know, this is a little thin. Do you think you can give us another 20,000 words?"

"No," said the business guru, who was then getting north of $50,000 a speech.

Nasty phone calls were exchanged back and forth and finally a meeting was arranged between the publisher's top people and the guru and his agent.

The conversation went like this:

PUBLISHER: If you don't give us another 10,000 words or so [you can see how quickly they backed down from their initial demand], I am afraid we are going to have to ask for our $1 million advance back.

GURU: (Reaching for his checkbook) Fine. (Pause.) By the way, if you pull my book off your list, what is going to be your lead title for spring?[3]

PUBLISHER: (Silence.)

Both sides stared across the table at one another for a while and then the guru's agent (who happened to be my agent as well) spoke up.

AGENT (to publisher): You know Paul B. Brown, right?

[They did. I had written a couple of books for them a few years back.]

AGENT: You like him. Right?

PUBLISHER: Right. [They should have. I made them a lot of money.]

AGENT (to guru): Paul is another client of mine, a good guy, and he is easy to work with. Why don't I hook the two of you up and see if Paul can help you create another fifty pages in a few weeks.

That's exactly what happened. About thirty days later the revised manuscript was on the way to production. [**E.K.: It's impressive how deftly you weave the shameless self-promotion into the meat of the text. You're lucky this book has a sense of humor (and that you're telling the truth).**]

And the Moral Is

There are a couple of messages you should take away from these stories:

First, publishers are reluctant to kill books.

Second, their reluctance is directly proportional to the visibility of the project. If they have more than $1 million tied up in a book, as

---

3. There is always at least one big book on a publisher's list. This book is expected not only to draw a lot of attention to itself but also to get people talking about other books that the publisher is bringing out.

in the case of the business guru, they are going to work really hard to make sure the book gets in the stores.

Third, you shouldn't count on points one and two. Figure in your case they won't have any major qualms about killing a book that they don't think lives up to their expectations because the odds say they didn't pay you $1 million.

It's like the old joke. If you owe the bank $200, it is your problem. If you owe the bank $200 million, it is the bank's problem. You are much more likely to be in the position of the first debtor than of the second. Since that is the case, it is important to know up front what the publisher's expectations are.

Yes, publishers are reluctant to kill books they have signed up. But they do it on occasion. What does this mean for you? That the Boy Scouts got it right. Hope for the best, but prepare for the worst.

Let me give you a checklist you can use in talking with your editor about his or her expectations for your book. As always, I think it would be swell if you could get the editor's position in writing, it will make life so much easier later on, should something go wrong.

In the checklist, be sure to ask your editor:

○ What material should be covered?

○ From whose point of view?

○ What audience are we trying to reach?

○ How should the material be presented in terms of tone (academic, colloquial), graphics (charts and tables), and style—is it okay to be a wise guy, or should you sound like your kindly old neighborhood doctor, or perhaps a techno-nerd?

○ How long should it be? (The answer should be in number of words and not pages.)

○ What is the real deadline?[4]

Keep all those thoughts in mind when you are going over the contract. Have everything spelled out in the contract—and hope for the best.

How the Publisher Plans on Selling the Book

As you go through the contract you receive from the publisher, you will notice something interesting. There are no specifics about how the publisher plans to promote the book. That was not an oversight on the publisher's part. Publishers hate talking about their marketing plans.

They will tell you it is because:

(a) You, the author, won't understand the intricacies of marketing plans.

(b) It is impossible to set a marketing budget a year (or more) ahead of when the book will be published.

(c) "Who knows what new media will be available by the time the book is published?"

---

4. What is in the contract, such as "the manuscript is due no later than June 30, 2004," is invariably not the real deadline. Editors build in a fudge factor. Why do you care? Because it gives the publisher one more potential reason for rejecting your manuscript.

Publishers know saying "cause I didn't like it" is not the world's strongest legal position when it comes to justifying the rejection of a manuscript. So, they look for other reasons, such as missing a deadline.

If they are looking for a reason to reject the manuscript that you turned in July 15, they will point to the June 30 deadline as justification, even if the real deadline they always had in mind was September 1. This is why you want to have the contract specify a real deadline date, if possible.

The reality is much simpler:

○ Publishers don't want you bugging them about the marketing of what you have written, especially if the book does not climb the bestseller list with a speed that would make Janet Evanovich or Sue Grafton envious.

○ Publishers are not very good at it.

First point first. When a book doesn't sell, authors typically blame their publishers. [**E.K.: Yes, it is a well-known fact that in every case in the history of publishing as we know it: When a book tanks it is, rather remarkably, *always* the publisher's fault.**] And one of the things they point to is the lack of marketing support their book received. If a publisher spells out its marketing plans ("We are going to spend $6,752.90 promoting your book"), you can bet that the author is going to track each and every dime that is and isn't spent, especially if sales are slow.

To get around the problem, publishers simply don't reveal what their marketing budgets are. As one editor told me during a lengthy discussion in a negotiation over a book that he really wanted from me: "If we didn't tell Stephen King what we were going to spend to promote his book—and we didn't—we certainly are not going to tell you."

On a superficial level all this makes sense. But if you spend more than twenty seconds thinking about it, you realize that the publisher is just blowing smoke.

First, they do have a real good sense of what they are going to spend supporting the book when they make the offer to buy it. Remember our discussion about how publishers buy books? The editor makes a recommendation to the editorial board, which has at least a couple members of the sales and marketing team as members. They factor in how many copies they think the book will sell, and how much they are going to spend promoting it, as part of determining how much they can offer you as an advance.

So they do have a really good handle on how they are going to market your book; in fact they have a marketing plan complete with tentative budget all drawn up somewhere, they just don't want to share it.

Is there another reason, then, why the publisher doesn't want to spell out their marketing plans? You bet. They are terrible marketers.

I have spent a lot of time studying marketing—I have written books on the subject and at one point served as marketing editor of *Business Week*—and I have always thought marketing at its core was pretty simple:

○ You figure out who you want to sell (your book, in this case) to.

○ Then you determine what it is going to take to get them (potential readers) to buy.

Publishers have never mastered either variable. Not only are they decades behind the mass marketers like P&G (Tide, Crest, Pampers) and Wal-Mart in terms of using technology to both track and predict sales, they are not very good at using the few resources they do have, as generations of authors have learned the hard way.

You don't need to take my word for this. Many of the books I have done involved working with CEOs, either helping them to write their books or editing what they have written. At some point in the process, usually after they complained about the publisher's plans for selling their book, the executive will turn to me and say, "You know if those folks worked in our marketing department, they would be gone by the end of the day."

So What Is an Author to Do?

All this is (hopefully) interesting, but it does not help you much. The question you (should) have is: "What do I have to do to ensure that my book gets more than its fair share of attention from the publisher?"

The following checklist should help:

○ *First, and foremost, talk to the editor.* After she says, "This (what you are about to write for them) is an important book for us," ask, "How important?" Is your book one of the publisher's lead books for the current list, meaning one of the ones that are most important to the publisher over the next three to six months, or is it there just to make sure all the bases are covered (to "round out the list," as they say in the business)? The more important the book is to the publisher, the more support it will receive. [**E.K.: Paul, you know perfectly well that all books don't *require* the same amount of support. Some books won't sell without a major push—but some books (like yours) can be expected to sell steadily for many years without the publisher placing ads in the *Wall Street Journal.*]** To paraphrase *Animal Farm* author George Orwell: "All books are equal, but some books are more equal than others."

○ *Ask: "What exactly are your marketing plans?"* While they won't give you a dollar amount, if the publisher is going to take out national advertisements in the *Wall Street Journal* or *USA Today*, you have a pretty good idea that your book is important to them. If they say, in essence, "We are going to wait and see what happens with the initial orders before we finalize our plans," then you know that it is not.

○ *Will you support the book once it does well?* Most book marketing has always struck me as being counterintuitive. Publishers will throw huge amounts of money against a sure thing—such as the new John Grisham book—and ignore first-time authors who need all the help they can get in breaking through the clutter. If you can't get a firm marketing commitment up front, at least try to get a promise that the publisher will throw some money behind your book once it starts to do well. (While Doubleday didn't do one darn thing to support *Customers for Life* until we sold 100,000 copies, they were terrific after we started popping up on bestseller lists.) How will you know your book is doing well? That is a great question. Not only do publishers not like to share marketing information, they hate to share sales information. If sales are slow, they don't like to deliver bad news. And if sales are good, authors are bound to ask for more marketing support to turn good sales into great ones.

As a result, the only real sales numbers you receive can be found in your royalty statement, and as we will discuss in a minute, those numbers are terribly out of date by the time you receive them.

But all is not lost when it comes to sales numbers. Technology has come to your rescue. All you have to do is visit Amazon.com or BN.com. (Since both sites work basically the same, we will use Amazon as the example.)

Once your book is published, it goes into Amazon's inventory of more than 3 million books, and while publishers are terrible and don't know what sells, Amazon is terrific at it. (They are both in the book business, go figure.) Once a week, Amazon.com updates the sales ranks of *its entire inventory.* The top 10,000 bestsellers are updated hourly, and the next 100,000, daily.

So, to find out how well your book is selling on Amazon, type its title into the Amazon.com search engine and then scroll down to "product details" where you'll see its rank among the 3,000,000 books.

Are Amazon's rankings representative of book sales as a whole? Pretty much. [**E.K.: Sometimes. Of course, rankings can fluctuate radically and often, and Amazon.com doesn't indicate how many copies were actually sold to achieve a ranking, so it can be misleading.**] So, if your publisher won't provide you with sales numbers, go to the Amazon site. And if your book is selling well over a long period of time, ask for even more marketing support. If it is not, use the consistently low numbers as a reason that your publisher needs to be doing more. There is no guarantee you will get what you ask for, but I can guarantee the odds are substantially less if you don't ask.

○ *How long will you give me?* Like cartons of milk, books have a fixed expiration date in a publisher's mind. They will support a book for only so long before they turn their attention elsewhere. You want to have an idea upfront how long that is.

The Party Is Over

Do you want to ask for a book tour or book publication party? You can, but it most likely will be a waste of your breath.

Up until the early 1990s, book tours were fairly common. The publisher would send the author on the road for a week, or two, or three, lining up interviews with as many newspapers and radio and television stations as possible. If you like to travel, it was actually fairly enjoyable. The publisher picked up the cost of everything, and there usually was a local guide to help you get about wherever the publisher sent you.

Those days are basically gone, victims of cost cutting and better technology that allows you to sit in a studio in New York and do one radio or television interview after another across the country, without leaving your seat.

As for book parties, they were fun, but the reality is they didn't sell any books—the people who attended left with free books (they would have been insulted if you asked them to pay), and they really didn't generate a whole lot of press—so they, too, have become an anachronism.

However, you should have a discussion of exactly what your publisher is willing to do for you.[5]

---

5. You can hire your own marketing/publicity firm, either as a supplement to what the publisher does or as a surrogate, should the publisher not be willing to lift a finger.

Hiring an outside marketing firm is fairly common, and some of them, such as the Hendra Agency in Brooklyn, New York, and Planned Television Arts out of Manhattan are very good. The problem is someone has to pay for this, and these folks don't come cheap. Figure $5,000 to $10,000 a month with a minimum of a three-month commitment on your part. That's why, whenever possible, you want the publisher to be picking up the tab.

You should try raising the issue of bringing in an outside marketing firm (and having the publisher pay for it). Odds are you won't get the publisher to write a check to hire one of these firms, but you might find you get a bit more internal support as a result. As my daughter learned when she was small, if you want a kitten start by asking for a pony.

How the Publisher Wants to Pay You

My buddy Carl Sewell may be the world's most charming man. The quintessential Southern gentleman, Carl, who was born, raised, and still lives in Dallas, can make anyone feel comfortable in any situation. Now there are some people who see the manners, and hear the soft-spoken style, and feel that they can take advantage of him, especially in a business situation.

No one ever has.

While Carl owns one of the nation's largest automobile dealers—his seventeen franchises do more than $1 billion in sales a year—he is quick to point out to people who try to take advantage of him that "I grew up on a used-car lot." (That is literally true. Carl's father started the business with one Cadillac dealership in Dallas, and Carl worked on the dealership's used-car lot during high school.)

Not only are publishers reluctant to pay you a lot of money up front, they will put off paying what they owe you just about until the point at which you are willing to threaten legal action.

Every time I negotiate a contract with a publisher, I wish I shared Carl Sewell's upbringing. As Carl, who has dealt with publishers twice, puts it: "These boys (publishers) would feel right at home on the used-car lot."

You wouldn't think that is the case. And it has nothing to do with the entire pretense that the book business is really about creating art, and people don't quibble about the price of art. First, it doesn't help you to think of your book as "art" and besides, even the best art galleries haggle all the time.

No, the real reason this is surprising is that you wouldn't think there would be much to haggle over.

If the publisher likes your idea and makes you an offer it will be:

(a) Fairly low—because you don't have much of a track record; therefore, you don't have a lot of leverage when it comes to demanding a huge up-front advance.

(b) Fairly close to the real amount the publisher wants to pay. The publisher might go up a tad to make you feel a little bit better, but it takes an awful lot of tads to pay the mortgage.

If this is the case, why do you need used-car-lot experience, which prepares you for the deviousness the world has to offer? That's easy. Even though what the publisher pays you is relatively small, they will put off paying it as long as possible. This takes numerous forms, as we will discuss, but let's start with the most basic example:

Let's say you receive an offer of $25,000 to write your book. (The publisher originally offered $20,000, but you got them up to $25,000.)

You might think you sign the contract promising to write the book and then the publisher gives you a check for $25,000.

Not a chance.

The best you can hope for when it comes to payment terms is: half the money up front—i.e., when you sign the contract—and the other half when the publisher "accepts" the manuscript, meaning, as we talked about before, they have read, and are happy with, what you have written.

"But wait," I hear you cry. "This means I have to wait a year (or however long it takes me to write the book) to get the rest of my money."

Yep, and it could get worse.

Some contracts say you get half the advance on signing, and the other half on publication—and remember that it can take a minimum of nine months from the time you turn the manuscript in until the book is published. In that case it would be twenty-one months (twelve months to write the book, plus another nine months to wait) until you got your money.

And even that is a better deal than the fairly typical offer of one-third on signing, one-third on acceptance, and one-third on publication. And it is certainly better than what is becoming all the rage among publishers (especially if they pay a lot of money up front): one-fifth on signing, one-fifth on acceptance of half the manuscript, one fifth on the entire book, one fifth on publication, and the final

fifth six months after publication. [E.K.: So that last part is not technically an "advance," right? Depending on the size of the advance
and the book's early sales, the first royalty check may arrive before
the fifth "advance" payment. Anyway, what are *you* complaining
about? At least you got more money than you should have up
front.]

Let's go back to your $25,000 advance. Under the last (one-fifth
five times) scenario, you would get $5,000 on signing (and actually
plan on a month after signing, since publishers pay slooooowly, no
matter how small or large the check). Another $5,000 when you have
completed half the book, which we will assume is in six months.
Another $5,000 six months later when the publisher accepts. Another
$5,000 nine months later upon publication, and the last $5,000 six
months after that.

This means that it takes twenty-seven months, or two and a quarter years, from the time you sign the contract until you get the last of
the money owed you from the advance.

In our example, that would work out to be less than $1,000 a
month. And that is assuming you get $25,000 to write your book.
Many first-time authors don't receive even that much. Do you still
want to write books?

But There Is Champagne on the Back End, No?

No.

As mentioned previously, you'll get some money up front. As
they say in the business, you'll be getting some sort of advance.

The word *advance* is really a shorthand way of saying "advance
against royalties."

Here's how royalties work, and why (again) you must pay careful
attention to the way the publisher words the payout clause.

Let's start at the beginning. A royalty, when we are talking about
book publishing, is nothing more than a fixed percentage of the suggested cover price for each copy sold.

Usually you receive 10 percent of the retail price on the first five thousand books sold—with some publishers the "first five thousand" can climb as high as 10,000 copies—and the percentage increases from there until it hits—and stays at—15 percent.[6] However, you don't see any royalties until the book has "earned out," meaning that it has recouped the advance the publisher has given you.

Let's go back to our example to see how this works.

Remember, we said you received an advance of $25,000, and we will assume when your book is published it will carry a $25 cover

---

6. Can you get the royalty rate to go higher than 15 percent? Conceivably yes, but probably not, and my recommendation would be to not even try.

Here's why. The moment you raise the issue of a higher royalty payment—perhaps in exchange for a smaller advance—the publisher is going to say, "It can't be done." They will begin by explaining that the 15% you are receiving is actually 30% of the gross paid to the publisher, since publishers sell books to bookstores at about 50% off the cover price.

With that as the starting point, the publisher will go on to say they won't be able to make any money on your book (and therefore implicitly threaten not to publish what you have written) if you demand more than 15% of royalties. A higher royalty would make publishing your book a money-losing proposition. **[E.K.: If not now, then later on when the printings are smaller and the unit manufacturing costs therefore higher.]**

The reality is the publisher could afford to pay you more, especially if you are willing to take little or no money up front. You can make the numbers work for you and the publisher, but you probably don't want to go through the hassle.

Here's why. If you insist on a bigger share of the royalties, the publisher is going to say "Fine, you can have a royalty rate of X% [with X being royalties as high as 50% of the cover price] after our expenses are covered." You'd be amazed, though, how high those expenses are going to be. Who knew you had to pay for the latte bought by the messenger who took your manuscript downstairs in the publisher's building and gave it to the typist who inputted what you wrote into the publisher's computer system.

And who is going be doing the accounting of those expenses? The publisher. Traditional royalty statements are frustrating enough. You don't want to compound the problem.

So, instead of trying to increase the royalty rate, see if you can get a larger advance. It will decrease your chance of getting an ulcer.

price. And let's also say—to keep the math simple—that the contract says you get 10 percent of the cover price for the first 10,000 copies, and 15 percent for each copy above that.

That means if you sell exactly 10,000 copies, you will be *credited* with having earned $25,000.

In other words, as the publisher records the sale of your 10,000th copy, they say, "Great, you have earned back all of the money we gave you. We shelled out $25,000. You've earned $25,000 so far—the 10 percent of the $25 cover price you would have received on those 10,000 books sold—so we are even."

So, on the first 10,000 copies you sell, you will receive no more additional money. If you reach 10,000 you have "earned out." Starting with the 10,001st copy sold, you will get $3.75 a book for each and every book you sell going forward.

What happens if you don't earn out? Absolutely nothing. You get to keep the advance. That explains why publishers try to pay advances that are as small as possible, and is a major reason authors try to get as much money as they possibly can up front.

Okay, you say, the idea is to get as much money up front. It's as simple as that, right?

Wrong.

Here are a few other things to ask about:

❍ *When do you start earning the maximum royalties per book?* You want it to occur as soon as possible—say, at 5,000 copies sold—but publishers will want it to take a while. They might suggest 15,000 copies being the trigger. Like every other term in the contract, this is negotiable, no matter what the publisher says initially.

❍ *What happens on paperback sales?* You might think the royalty rate would remain the same. If the publisher has its way, it won't. What typically happens is if the paperback rights are sold—that is, someone agrees to bring out a paperback version of your book—the publisher is considered to be an equal partner with you. So instead of getting 15 percent of sales, you get 7.5 percent and the publisher gets

7.5 percent. And you get 7.5 percent even if the publisher holds onto the book in paperback and publishes the soft-cover version itself. Obviously, the higher the percentage of the paperback royalties you receive, the more money you will make. [**E.K.: Paul, you're forgetting that since the retail price of the paperback is much lower while the manufacturing cost remains substantially the same, the publisher's profit margin shrinks. By having a lower royalty rate you're helping the publisher keep your book** *in print.*] Sheesh!

○ *What are they going to hold back for reserves?* This is one of my pet peeves, one a lot of authors share. Royalties are based on the number of books sold. But since publishers are still using accounting and inventory tracking technology that was already out of date in the 1980s, they don't know for certain how many copies of your book were sold, or, in fact, if any were sold. They only know how many they shipped. And so, in calculating royalties, they take the number of books they have sent to retailers, subtract how many of them they think will be returned—almost always a retailer can return unsold books after a certain length of time—and pay you a royalty on the difference. You understand the problem. The higher the reserve, the less they will pay you. [**E.K.: I think you should point out that six months later in the next royalties period, the publisher does credit the author's royalty account with only money it held in reserve for the previous period.**] Given existing technology, the reserve should be zero. That said, if they have a reserve of more than 10 percent of the books shipped, scream and try to negotiate a lower number. [**E.K.: Just as long as your readers know that the reserve percentage is frequently much higher than 10 percent, even though you don't think it should be. (I can live with the screaming.)**]

○ *When are they going to pay you?* This is actually what prompted Carl Sewell to make his remark about publishers knowing their way around the used-car lot in the first place. The way AMACOM pays royalties—twice a year—is typical in the industry. It is no wonder Carl was frustrated. Say it is January 2, and someone's New Year's resolution was to buy the book you had written. Assuming the book had already "earned out," when would you receive payment for that book purchased January 2? Somewhere around Thanksgiving. Why? Under terms of the contract, the reporting period ends June 30. And then the publisher has four months to issue a check. [**E.K.: Worth noting that AMACOM pays you within *two* months, but your main point is well taken.**] What happens is the publisher waits until the absolute last second—midnight October 31 in this case—before posting the check in apparently the most obscure mailbox it can find. My checks always seem to show up seven days—November 7, in this case— after the postmarked date. Now the situation I just described is *the best-case scenario.* I'll give you an example of how it can get worse—much worse.

In May 2002, authors who had written books for one of the largest publishing houses on the planet went to their mailboxes expecting a royalty check for the period ending the previous December 31, but instead they found a letter that said, in order to serve its authors better, the publisher had installed a new accounting system, and "well, you know how these things go; it is taking longer than expected so, yes, we know we owe you money, but, no, we have no idea when you are going to get it and don't even think about calling us to complain." (The quote is not exact, but that was the message.)

I didn't think much of the fact that my check was delayed—I am used to the fact that the people in publishing get paid every two weeks and authors get money when the publishers feel like it. But I did have the letter in the back of my mind when a couple of months later I signed a contract with the same large publishing house to do an update of a book that I had written for them years before that was continuing to sell, but was now a bit stale.

They agreed to pay $20,000 for the update and paid fairly quickly.

I got that payment in March—three months after the preceding royalty statement was to have closed.

Yet, when I finally got my long overdue royalty statement for the period ending the previous December 31, the publisher had somehow managed to record the check they had sent me in March. So instead of owing me $12,000—which they had, thanks to the $20,000 payment, a payment that by all rights should not have been recorded for another three months—I owed them money. Instead of having $32,000 in hand—the $20,000 for the update, and the $12,000 I was owed for past royalties—I only had the $20,000. They had successfully managed to put off paying me the other $12,000.

Is it too late to learn my way around the used-car lot?

What We Have Learned

While there are several variations on the theme, the basic point about this is simple: Publishers will pay you as little as they can—both up front and in terms of royalties—and they will put off paying whatever they owe for as long as possible.

Saying that shouldn't be the case doesn't help anyone. It is the case, and you need to know it going in.

What can you do about it? A lot, I contend, such as the following:

1. *Insist on the largest advance possible.* When the publisher asks, "Don't you share our vision of the book's potential," and then goes on to suggest that you take a smaller advance so that they can spend more up front to promote the book, say, "Yes, of course, I believe in the book. I wrote it." But then insist on the largest advance you can. First, since publishers take forever to pay royalties, you will be at least assured of having something up front to show for all your hard work. And second, the more money they pay out initially, the more (ironically?) they will do to promote what you have written. Strange, but true. If they give you a $10,000 advance and your book doesn't sell, the publisher just takes a $10,000 hit. No big deal for a multi-million-dollar publisher. However, if they give $1 million and the book tanks, then the editor and publisher have a lot of explaining to do. They will work really hard to make that book a bestseller.

2. *Remember: everything is negotiable.* And "everything" means everything. [**E.K.: Not** *here* **it doesn't.**] Not only are the size of the advance and how the royalties are to be paid open to discussion—despite the publisher's first reaction that they have absolutely no intention of haggling over this or anything else—but so is the time the book is to be delivered as well as how the book will be marketed. If you don't like a term in the contract the publisher sends you, talk to your editor about it and keep talking about it until you reach terms you both can live with.

3. *Negotiate mutual penalties for noncompliance.* One of the most intriguing parts of the standard publishing contract is that the entire onus is on you, the writer. You can be penalized, and there are no sanctions against publishers for either doing something wrong or failing to live up to their word. That isn't fair, but you can try to balance the playing field. You can negotiate into the contract penalties (the lawyers call them "liquidated damages") that will be assessed if the publisher fails to do what they promised. For example, if your royalty checks are late, you should get interest on the time you are forced to wait for your money, or if the publisher says they will do a, b, c, d, e, and f to support your book, and they only do "b," you should receive a check to compensate for the potentially lost sales their failure caused. Publishers will tell you that they never agree to liquidated damages clauses. That just isn't the case. I have had the clause inserted into various contracts I have done. Now, again, first-time authors may not have the leverage to have these clauses inserted, but it is definitely worth pursuing.

Why Would You Want to Compound the Problem?

Not only does the publisher want to take control over this book, they want a shot at your next one as well.

Invariably, the contract you receive will have a clause giving the publisher the right to publish your next book. You understand why it is there. If book #1 is a huge hit, they will want to publish book #2.

But the danger from your point of view is equally clear. You have no idea how the experience of publishing the first book with them is going to go, and here they are asking for control over your second book, when it is more than possible that they will have made your experience getting the first one published a living hell. (You won't know about the publisher's actions until you actually turn in the manuscript and they edit it and try to sell it. These are things that could be a year or two away.)

What do you do today when they are asking you to sign an option for your second book?

Well, of all the changes to a contract, eliminating or modifying this option is probably the easiest.

If the publisher won't drop the option clause outright, try to insist on language that will either soften it substantially, or at least compensate you for having it there in the first place. [**E.K.: Our option clause is already so soft it oozes.**]

For example, you might try to get the option to say that the publisher has an option, providing you and he can reach "mutually agreeable terms." If you don't agree with what the publisher is offering in terms of money, or how the publisher wants to approach the material that will be contained in your second book, then you can say, "Thanks, but no thanks, we need to part company when it comes to me writing book number two."

Or you can try to get the publisher to pay you a reasonable sum of money to have a first look at what you want to say in your next book. Suggesting that is usually enough for them to consider dropping the option clause.

Bargaining away the right governing who is going to publish your next book is not something you want to do without spending a lot of time thinking about it. The option is usually presented as the last clause in the contract, as if it is an afterthought. It is anything but.

Summing Up

After writing books for twenty years, I am absolutely convinced that not thinking about who controls the publishing process is the biggest source of unhappiness that authors—whether they are first-time or established—have. It always seems to come as a shock to them. It shouldn't.

You don't have a lot of leverage, especially if you are trying to get your first book published. But you do have some. (The publisher does want your book, after all; that is a huge plus, something you shouldn't forget.) Spend a lot of time trying to get a deal you can live with.

CHAPTER 7

You've Finished the Manuscript— Now What?

Notice that we have made a huge leap from the end of Chapter 6, where we discussed putting the final touches on the sale of your idea, to the beginning of this chapter. The part we skipped over? Writing the actual book.

That should have come as no surprise. Remember what we said at the beginning. We are taking as a given that you have something to say and you know how to say it. And clearly if you have gotten this far in the publishing process, at least one editor must have expressed confidence in your ability to turn in a finished manuscript. How do we know? They have just offered you a contract.

So, assuming you have a contract that you can live with, a fact that you have indicated by signing it, what happens next?

Well, you have to write the silly book.

But what about all the stuff that happens before that? The boozy dinner with your editor where the two of you talk long into the night about each of your expectations for the book and how you plan to celebrate when it climbs the bestseller lists. Won't that take place? Probably not. Those scenes occur only in (bad) fiction or (even worse) movies about the publishing business. **[E.K.: True. But**

then, there *is* that pineapple cheesecake that I've promised to bake you. Dianne, my excellent and trustworthy assistant, will vouch for the fact that it is a far better prize than even the most fiction-perfect celebratory supper.]

The reality is once you sign the contract, you may never hear from your editor again until you turn in your manuscript. That's isn't hyperbole. It's a fact.

Most of the time this silence is unintentional. There always seems to be a crisis du jour in an editor's life, and someone who is writing a book that isn't due for a year or more can quickly fall off the editor's radar screen as she wrestles with problems that need to be solved today.

But sometimes the neglect *is intentional.*

Once, when asked at a writers' conference what his ideal relationship would be with an author, a big-deal editor responded: "The dream relationship? The writer drops off what can only be described as the perfect manuscript, not one thing needs to be changed, and then he leaves our offices, walks outside, and is hit by a bus."

The editor was kidding.

I think.

After you sign your book contract, you may not hear from your editor until you turn in your manuscript. Depending on your perspective, this is not necessarily a bad thing.

The takeaway message about this is clear. Once you have signed the book contract, you are probably not going to hear from your editor for a while.

Is that a good thing or a bad one?

It depends on your point of view.

Personally, I like it. A quick story will tell you how I prefer to deal with editors.

I did my second and third books with Harriet Rubin, who as I said was the hot nonfiction editor in the 1980s and into the 1990s. She did

books with everyone from David Stockman, a key Ronald Reagan lieu-
tenant, to businesspeople such as Max Dupree (*Leadership Is an Art)* to
global-thinking academics like Peter Senge (*The Fifth Discipline).* For
about a decade, Harriet's books dominated the nonfiction bestseller
lists. She was so successful that Doubleday created an imprint just for
her, called Doubleday/Currency, which exists to this day.

Harriet was unusual in a lot of ways. For one thing, it seemed she
commissioned more books—that is, she came up with an idea and
then set out to find someone to write it—than she bought (from people
sending her query letters and book proposals). She would decide that
a CEO—such as John Sculley, the previous head of PepsiCo, who in
the late 1980s was running Apple Computer—had a story to tell, and
she would convince that CEO to write a book. No proposal necessary.
She would even help the author find a writer to help tell the story, if
that would make him or her more comfortable. (Sculley did his book
with then–*Business Week* senior writer John A. Byrne, who is now the
editor-in-chief of *Fast Company.)*

Perhaps because she went after so many nontraditional authors,
she had an unusual way of dealing with all of them. She would actually talk to us from time to time.

After I signed with Harriet to write *Marketing Masters,* a book
that we sketched out over a long (no-alcohol-was-consumed) lunch,
she gave me a call.[1] Once the obligatory pleasantries were exchanged,
here's how the conversation went.

---

1. In case you care, and the underwhelming sales of the book indicates you probably
don't, *Marketing Masters: Lessons in the Art of Marketing* was what both Harriet and
I thought was a good idea. In essence, it was six long magazine pieces, each one
focusing on what I thought was one of the best marketing companies in the United
States at that time (the late 1980s)—Victoria's Secret (owned by The Limited); South-
western Bell, which had just introduced a Yellow Pages aimed at people over age 60
called, logically enough, "the Silver Pages"; Worlds of Wonder (they made Laser Tag
and Teddy Ruxpin); PepsiCo; Merrill Lynch; and Godfather's Pizza. What tied them all
together were common themes revolving around customer focus and the willingness
to change with the times.

Book buyers were underwhelmed by the premise, and Harriet's employer at the time,
HarperCollins, which was called Harper & Row back then, was underwhelmed by
the sales. The book sank without a trace.

HARRIET: How do you like to work?

ME (articulate as ever): Huh?

HARRIET: Well, some writers need a phone call each morning to help them get up and remind them to get to work. If you are one of them, I can have my assistant do it every day. Others like to send in a chapter or two after they have completed it. Others like to wait until they have finished half the book, and there are some writers who . . .

ME: Oh, I get it. Well, if it is all the same to you, I'd just as soon write the whole thing and send it to you when I am done, since you already have a pretty good idea of what I am going to do.

HARRIET: Fine.

I set off to write the book, which was due in twelve months. I was writing the book during nights, weekends, and slow days at the office—I was a staff writer and marketing columnist at *Inc.* at the time—and I didn't think any more about the conversation. Harriet said she wouldn't call, and she didn't.

One day my phone rang.

HARRIET: I know I promised I wouldn't call until the year was up [it had been about eleven and a half months], but I wanted to see whether you will meet the deadline. I am writing the catalog copy. I just wanted to make sure it was okay to include your book.

ME: I will have the finished manuscript to you next week.

While I was happy Harriet called, I really wouldn't have thought less of her if she hadn't. I don't expect a lot of interactions with editors. Having spent five years working in the city room of a major metropolitan daily (as they used to say on *Superman*) and surviving another five years at the Marine boot camp that is known as *Forbes* magazine—a place where people used to be routinely fired on Christmas Eve—I truly don't know what to do when confronted with a warm and fuzzy editor. [**E.K.: That explains a lot of things.**]

But that's me. I like working on my own. Since I am not cursed with self-doubt [**E.K. writes: Truer words were never written.**], it almost never occurs to me that the editor is not going to like what I turn in. And in fact, I find discussing ahead of time what I want to do to be somewhat inhibiting.

The First Answer Is Usually No

It is always easier for editors—as well as human beings, who editors sometimes resemble—to reject ideas, especially new ideas, than to embrace them whole-heartedly. [**E.K.: As someone who not infrequently resembles a human, I protest!**] And that is definitely true if those ideas are presented in the abstract.[2] So when I am writing a book, I find it is better just to present the material in question in the way I want, instead of talking about the idea up front. If the editor likes it, swell. If not, I can always change it.[3]

But, again, that is just me. I am willing to risk the rejection. [**E.K.: Because you're so used to it?**] I'll do this because:

○ I write quickly, so coming up with something new won't take too much time.

○ I figure I will be able to salvage something out of what I submitted, so even if the editor says no, it won't be a total loss.

However, I know most people don't want to work this way. Most writers want more interaction with their editors.

For one thing, they want to know if they are on the right track as they set off to write their book. Unlike me, they are quite correctly worried about wasting time.

2. For a great list of examples, go unearth the old George Gershwin song "They All Laughed," which begins with the lyric: "They all laughed at Christopher Columbus. . . ."

3. This is just a variation on the Brown family motto: It is always easier to apologize than to get permission.

There are some editors (like this fellow) who will hang on your every word. Unfortunately, they are the exceptions.

For another, they want the editor's input so that she feels more invested in the project, and sometimes they just crave human contact. For some people, the process of writing books can be equal to lying in a sensory deprivation tank.[4]

Without that contact, some people go—for lack of a more precise term—nuts.

---

4. I have four kids, a peripatetic wife, and a 90-pound dog with attention deficit disorder (ADD), so a sensory deprivation tank is something I would love, if you are wondering what to get me for Christmas.

Editor/Writer Relations

There was once a potential author, an expert in his field, who felt compelled to explain an arcane part of his profession to the world in the form of a book.

With some help from a terrific agent, he crafted a great proposal and got his idea sold to one of the nation's largest publishers for a low six-figure advance.

And then he never heard from his editor.

At first, the new author was happy to chalk up the lack of contact to the editor being busy. And then when a couple of more weeks went by—and his phone calls were still not returned—he assumed his editor was on vacation. But when it had been months since he had heard from anyone associated with his publisher, he basically flipped out. He started assuming that the editor did not want the book he had signed up.

Convinced that was the case, the author went off in a totally new direction, one that the editor absolutely hated when he saw the manuscript.[5]

So communication can be a good thing. And a lack of it can lead to all kinds of negative surprises in addition to someone going nuts. For example, it can result in you producing a book that the editor doesn't want.

When that happens, there are only three options, and none of them are particularly attractive from an author's point of view.

1. First, the editor is going to ask you to do extensive rewrites. Although this is painful—after all, you thought you were essentially done once you turned in the manuscript—it is the most pleasant of the three options that you could face.

---

5. I know about this only because I was called in to try to save it. But by that time, it was too late. What the author had created was basically 80,000 stream-of-consciousness words about his field. If there were a book somewhere inside those ramblings, I never found it. Apparently, no one else did either. As far as I know, the book was never published.

2. If more severe changes are needed, the editor will either rewrite what you have written or hire someone like me to do it. If the editor does it, you may not recognize the end result. If the editor decides someone from the outside is needed— because she doesn't have the time to do it—not only might you not recognize the end result, you may end up paying for the book doctor's time.

3. If it is hopeless, the editor will kill the book.

So if you have any doubts about the direction your book will take, or which route you will take to get it there, you want to ensure there is a lot of communication with your editor.

What must you do to ensure that this communication takes place? Talk to your editor the moment the contract is signed. Say you want to have regular interaction, and perhaps set up the schedule right then and there. (Maybe you want to spend thirty minutes on the telephone the first Monday of every month, and you want to send the editor one finished chapter at a time, or whatever both of you are comfortable with.)

This is a good idea if you are at all skittish about the writing process. It can also be particularly important because of one of the many dirty secrets in publishing: Editors don't truly edit.[6]

Strange, but true.

How the Editing Process Works

If you go back to the discussion of the creation of the proposal in Chapter 5, you can understand why editors don't edit in the way we

---

6. Yes, of course, there are exceptions to this rule. Some editors deliberately take on only a limited number of books so they can devote a great deal of attention to each one [**E.K.: Regrettably, this is seldom an option for most editors.**], and, especially at some of the smaller publishing houses, editors will take a great deal of time with each book on their list.

However, both these instances are now the exception to the rule.

Overall, an editor's workload is increasing, which means, by necessity, the amount of time he or she can devote to each book is decreasing.

traditionally think of the word—someone rewriting sentences and moving text around.

As we have seen, editors have to turn out a lot of books in a given year—one every two and half weeks is not out of the ordinary at the typical large publishing house. As a result, not only can they not afford the time to look at a finished manuscript before they decide to buy a book, as we talked about in discussing the importance of creating a terrific proposal, they don't even have much time to devote to a finished manuscript once it is turned in.

They will give what you send them a quick skim, but their thinking process as they go over your manuscript is strictly binary: Can I live with what I have here or not?

If they can, they will go back and read your entire manuscript quickly and flag large issues—such as "Can you provide some support/background here?" or "Do you think what you have in Chapter 4 would work better in the second half of Chapter 1?"—and point out typos if they happen to catch them. Other than that, it is off to production. (More on that in a second.)

If they can't live with what you sent, odds are the editor will take one serious pass at identifying what is wrong. Again, she won't edit per se, but will send you a letter that sounds something like this:

Dear Author:

Thanks for your manuscript, which I really enjoyed reading. While I think you have made a promising start, there are a few spots in which a little more is needed and other places in the text that probably need to be reordered. . . .

And from there, the editor will tell you the chapters don't seem to be in any logical sequence, details are lacking, and your conclusion is weak. In general the editor will leave you with the impression that what you have written is a total piece of garbage.

And then the letter will conclude with something such as the following:

I don't think these changes/revisions will be overly time consuming. In addition to these comments, please take a careful look at additional specific notes I've made on pages throughout the manuscript, especially where I ask for additional examples. [The best editors will indeed give you some notes and point out specific flaws in addition to the general ones.]

You then will have a reasonable amount of time to basically rewrite the book. Once you do, the editor will go through the same binary process—Is it publishable or not?—again.

If it is not publishable even after you have revised it, there are only two options left: a massive rewrite by the editor, or someone else, to salvage what you have, or the editor will decide to kill your book.[7] Let's take a look at both paths, starting with the worst-possible scenario.

As discussed in Chapter 6, editors don't like to kill books. It would be nice to think that their reluctance has everything to do with appreciating the effort you put into creating your manuscript, but that is barely a factor in their decision to hold off killing a book for as long as possible. Editors see the decision not to publish what you turned in as a negative reflection on them. It tells the world they had bad judgment (in signing your book in the first place) and lack skill (otherwise the editor would have been able to "save" the book, right?); and it makes the editor look bad in front of his or her colleagues and in the industry.

Worse, as we discussed earlier, if an editor decides to kill a book once it is in the catalog—the publisher's list of upcoming books for sale—he generates ill will among the publisher's sales force, which was counting on the commissions that selling the book would bring in, and retailers, who had a space reserved on their shelves for the work.

---

7. If you have come fairly close to solving all the problems with your rewrite, your editor may give you a chance to revise it again. But don't count on it. Editors are reluctant to give up control this late in the publishing process. The odds are, by this time, she has already listed the book in the next catalog, and as we are about to see, it is incumbent on the editor at this point to make sure the book is out on time.

In short, when an editor kills a book, his reputation suffers. As a result, the editor has less credibility the next time he pitches a book to the editorial board or to the sales force. And editors with little credibility soon find themselves unemployed.

Given all this, editors are extremely reluctant to kill books. But they will.

[E.K.: I don't entirely agree with a number of things you've said in the last four paragraphs, Paul, but rather than interrupt you every few lines, I'll let our readers enjoy the melodrama.]

If it happens to you, find out exactly what the editor didn't like—the editor will be far more candid after making the decision not to publish than he was when giving you comments while you were working on the book. That shouldn't be surprising. After all, the editor no longer needs to worry about hurting your feelings. And despite the fact that the editor has decided not to publish what you have written, he will probably be sincere in wishing you "good luck placing the book with another house" and be willing to provide some guidance about what might make your book appeal to another publisher.

You want to have those comments in front of you, if you are thinking of taking your book elsewhere; they will give you something concrete to work with as you begin revising your manuscript.

And revising should be an option because of the following:

○ You have already done a lot of work on your book and it would be silly to scrap it at this point.

○ You have the option to sell it elsewhere.

By killing the book, the publisher—by definition—has given up any claims on it, so you are free to try to sell it elsewhere. If you succeed, your original publisher will ask you to repay your advance out of the proceeds of the sale to the new publisher. Whether you actually have to give the money back is an open question if it was not addressed by the contract that you signed with your first publisher—and often it is not. **[E.K.: "If and only if," Paul. Not all publishers**

can afford to write off millions of dollars in advances every few years.]

Just because they ask for the money back doesn't mean you have to give it them. **[E.K.: Don't start *that* again.]** Resolving this is a job for either your agent—if you have one—or a lawyer who specializes in publishing matters. Since these talks may get heated, you probably don't want to handle the negotiations yourself.[8]

Moving On

But let's think happier thoughts and assume your book is accepted, either by the first publisher or a second.

What happens then? Given what we have talked about so far, you won't be surprised to learn the answer is "not much." You'll get some broad suggestions from your editor about how you might want to improve things, and he may or may not send you the manuscript to deal with these comments before it moves on to copyediting.

---

8. What happens if you can't, or decide not to, resell your book after the publisher has rejected it? Do you have to pay back the advance? In all reality, probably not. And that is probably true even if there is a clause in the publishing contract that you signed that says you must.

Letting you keep the advance is not largesse on behalf of the publisher, it is just bowing to the inevitable. In the history of publishing, it is unlikely that any writer has ever saved even a nickel out of any advance. Indeed, as generations of barkeeps and landlords can attest, the advance usually has been pledged before the money has been received. So, the odds are the advance is long gone by the time the publisher asks for it back. And to be honest, they would be shocked if they recovered even 50 cents on the dollar. **[E.K.: Not so fast, Paul; at AMACOM we've had quite a few honorable authors return their advances.]**

The odds say the costs of trying to recover what you owe them will be far greater than anything the publisher could squeeze out of you.

As a compromise, publishers sometimes will say, "Fine, we know you don't have any of the advance left, so we will take what you owe us out of the next book that you do for us." But frequently, there is no next book that the publisher wants, or by the time there is an idea that looks promising, everyone at the publishing house has moved on to another job and has forgotten about this compromise agreement.

The net result is you are probably off the hook; you are able to keep the advance you have been paid. (But this is also another reason why publishers are reluctant to pay large advances.)

(If the editor doesn't kick the manuscript back to you, the expectation will be that you will deal with his comments in the copyedited version.)

Here's a trick of the trade. When your manuscript is about to be edited, include a note that describes in detail the things you really don't want changed. If the items are at all reasonable, they probably won't be.

The copyedited version? What's that?

Well, since editors don't spend much time editing, there is another layer in the production process called copyediting.[9] The copy editor will carefully read what you have written. They will be looking to see if it makes sense—you referred to King George II in Chapter 4, and fifty pages later, the same guy is now George III—and they will do the editing for spelling and grammar. (Most book editors, like most book writers, are actually pretty bad at grammar and wouldn't know a noun in direct address or subordinate conjunction if they tripped over one. And a significant number aren't good spellers.) **[E.K.: You could at least exempt me from this faintly damning (though accurate) generalization; I do get enough grief here about being a stickler on such matters. (Here's hoping someone is copyediting my comments.)]**

Now, I like copy editors. They have skills—like knowing when

---

9. It is also possible that you might be confronted by someone who is identified as a "line editor." Like bald eagles, white tigers, and other endangered species, there are not many of them left, but they still inhabit some publishing houses.

In essence, a line editor is a cross between an acquisition editor and a copy editor. Unlike the editor you deal with initially, the line editor doesn't spend any time acquiring books and very little, if any, dealing with writers face-to-face or on the phone. Like a copy editor, she only works on completed manuscripts.

But where the copy editor's charge is strictly defined as determining if the content and grammar of what you wrote make sense, the line editor's charge is broader and includes style and approach. This is often referred to as "development" work.

to use a comma—that I have never mastered. But even given that their jobs require them to be nitpickers, they sure pick a lot of nits. They will question you about everything from style—"Are you sure you want to be colloquial?"—to anything that could be remotely sensitive to anyone, anywhere, at anytime. ("On page 36, you referred to the New England Patriots playing a 'plain vanilla zone defense' in the Super Bowl against the St. Louis Rams. Are you sure you want to use the expression 'plain vanilla'? It could be perceived as an insult to White Anglo-Saxon Protestants.")[10]

Take their comments with several grains of salt. While it is always a good idea to take your editor's (or line editor's) comments extremely seriously—going so far as to drop him a note to explain why you don't think dividing Chapter 3 into two parts is the way to go, or why you don't believe splicing Appendix II to the back of Chapter 4 is going to help the reader much—you don't have to be as explicit when dealing with a copy editor.

They will write their remarks in the form of notes in the margin of your manuscript. Just below their comments, you can write them back saying, "I think saying 'plain vanilla' is okay. Let's leave it." Be polite, but firm.

Editing Step-by-Step

Since we have referred obliquely to getting comments back from editors, let's go through the editing process in detail. Why? Because the things that you would expect to happen probably won't.

For example, you might expect that you drop off a disk containing your manuscript, or e-mail the finished book—either each individual chapter, or in one big zip file—once you are done. That may happen. But then, it may not.

For example, nearly twenty years ago when I finished my first

---

10. I did not make up either comment. I actually received both queries—in separate books—from two different copy editors. I thanked them politely for their comments and left everything unchanged. All White Anglo-Saxon Protestants who are offended by my chatty tone can reach me at PaulBBrown@aol.com.

book, *Sweat Equity,* I carefully copied all the individual chapters onto two 5.25-inch disks (I told you this was twenty years ago) and proudly presented the disks one bright Monday morning to my editor's assistant at Simon & Schuster.

"What's this?" she said, looking at the disks.

"It's my book," I said, with all the pride a first-time author can muster.

"Oh, no," she said. "The only people who have word processors are in legal."

The story is *not* a cute anachronism. While just about every editor that you deal with today will have a computer on her desk, many will not be able to accept your manuscript electronically. They will ask for a printed version. They will want to have it keystroked into their computer system, instead. So, you give them a printed version, and eventually, someone at the publishing house will end up retyping what you turned in. Honest. **[E.K.: Actually, Paul, many editors ask for both electronic and hard copies. Believe it or not, not everyone edits on screen.]**

But before that happens, the editor will doodle her suggestions in the margins of the hard copy. If the changes or suggestions are substantial, the editor will send the printed-out version back to you—after someone has made a copy of it—and wait for you to incorporate the changes.

Once you do, the editor will ask you to print out another version, which he or she will read. And at some point, the editor will send the printed version—which may or may not contain additional comments—to a copy editor. (If the editor has added questions, you deal with them when you get the copyedited manuscript back.)

Again, the copy editor will read it for content—checking to see whether everything seems to make sense—and for grammar and style, and at some point someone will send you back what are called "first pass pages," meaning that the publisher, which in this case means your editor and copy editor, have taken a first pass at what you gave them and marked up the manuscript with questions, comments, and style changes.[11] Do you have to accept all the changes and answer every question? No. But common sense and common courtesy should come into play.

Contrary to what even many established writers believe, editors don't suggest making changes to a manuscript simply to annoy the author.

You have to assume that editors and copy editors are not suggesting changes to your prose because they have nothing better to do, or because they are trying to justify their paychecks. And the odds are they are not doing it because they want *their* prose to live on through the ages embedded in your book. (If immortality were their goal, they would write their own darn books.)

No, misguided though their suggested changes may be in your eyes, they are probably well intended. Consider them as such. You don't have to accept them all—if it is sufficiently serious, the editor will make the change again in a later version, after you have taken it out—but you do have to think about them all.

After you send the manuscript back with your changes to their changes—like theirs, yours will be written in the margins—odds are the book will be retyped once again by someone in the publishing house and the process will be repeated for a second time, and you will then receive "second pass pages," which you deal with in exactly the same way.

Once everyone is happy, bound galleys—a cheap-looking paperback-type book (with no cover art—unless yours is a "lead" book)—

---

11. Style in this case means the publishing house's style. Do they like to spell out the word "percent" instead of using the percentage symbol? Are they fond of putting a comma before the word *and*? It's that sort of thing. Different publishing houses handle these issues in different ways.

You might have noticed that we haven't mentioned the subject of fact-checking. There is a reason for that. The publisher is generally not going to do it.

If you want to guarantee that what you wrote is correct, you will have to do the checking yourself, or find someone to do it for you. Any and all mistakes—other than typos—will be yours and not your publisher's.

are created out of the manuscript. This will show you how the words will appear on the page once the book is actually printed. Each galley page is identical to a finished book page. This is your last chance to catch typos and to update anything that needs updating.

While you are working on the galleys, the marketing department is sending it out to the appropriate places for reviews. (More on that process in Chapter 8.)

How Long Does All This Take?

Everything we have talked about makes it sound as if editing is a long, elaborate, time-consuming process. And it is. The back-and-forth work on the manuscript can easily take a couple of months, and that is on top of the time it takes for the editor to turn her attention to your manuscript in the first place.

As pleasant as it would be to think the editor is waiting for your manuscript, and will drop everything once it arrives, the reality is much more mundane. Think of an editor's job as processing manuscripts as they come down an assembly line. When yours comes in, it takes its place at the end of the line. The editor will get to it when she gets to it, and it could easily take a month before that happens. The clock starts ticking when the editor first reads what you sent in, not when you send it in. [E.K.: I'd like to add that the amount of time it takes for a manuscript to be read is also a function of the book's projected publication date—so if a book is scheduled for later in

the season it may actually take more than a month for your editor to get to it, and that's nothing to worry about.]

So it may have been a month or more before the editing process starts and it could be another three until it is finished. And then from the time the galleys are printed until the books are actually in the stores can be a few months more.

All in all, count on at least nine months from the time you turn the manuscript in until there are "finished" (that is, actual) books available for sale.

Let's Think of Something to Do While We're Waiting

The temptation might be to do very little during this nine-month process. After all, for most of this time, it is going to be hurry up and wait. You will go weeks at a time without hearing anything, and then (usually with no advanced warning) a large package will show up at your door and you will be given only a couple days to review your editor's comments, respond as appropriate, and get the entire manuscript back to your publisher.[12]

But waiting passively is the worst thing you can do during this time. Your focus should turn to figuring out the best way to market and sell your book.

Those are the subjects of our next chapter.

---

12. Ask for your publisher's overnight service account number so that you can bill the mailing of the packages to them.

CHAPTER 8

Helping Your Publisher to Help You (Or Why You Must Be an Integral Part of Your Publisher's Marketing/P.R./Sales Process, Even if You Hate the Idea and Couldn't Sell a Box of Girl Scout Cookies to Your Mother if Your Life Depended on It)

This chapter deals with the single biggest mistake every author—first-time or longtime—makes. Authors don't work hard enough to sell their books once the books come off the presses.

There are a couple of explanations for why that is the case.

The first one concerns the way that most authors think about selling. By the time their book is being edited, these authors believe the days of having to sell their book are long behind them. They sold their book—to the publisher. They feel that was a big deal. And they are absolutely right. So, once the publisher buys the book, these authors believe their work is done.

"After all," they say, "the publisher has a sales and marketing staff to get it into the hands of people who buy books. I write them. They sell them. The selling process doesn't have one blessed thing to do with me."

Second, they don't like to sell. "If I wanted to go into sales, I would have become a salesperson," is the way they put it. "I'd be out selling, instead of trying to write books."

With apologies to greeting card writers everywhere: Completing your book is not the end of the successful book publishing journey. It is only the beginning.

Because of reason #1 or #2 or both, most authors don't give the sales and marketing of their book a thought beyond:

○ "What will the cover look like?"

○ "Is the publisher going to pay for a huge publication party?"

○ "What should I wear when they book me on *Oprah*?"

If *you* take that approach, and leave every aspect of the marketing of your book to other people, I can tell you how to save a lot of money: Don't buy any new clothes. You are not going to be asked to appear on *Oprah*. Heck, you may not even get a mention in the free local weekly newspaper that they give away down at the supermarket.

Yes, if you build a better mousetrap (or write a better book in this case), the world will beat a path to your door. But before they can start trooping down your front walk, trampling your flowers in the process, they need to *know* you have written a better book.

And the only way that is going to happen is through marketing.

Fine, you (grudgingly) concede, but "Why do I have to get involved with the marketing?"

There are a couple of reasons, including the following.

○ Who is going to do a better job than you? Who knows the content better? And, perhaps more important, who has the biggest vested interest in the success of your book? (a) Your editor, who has nineteen more books to publish this year? (b) Your publisher's marketing department, which is dealing with even more books than your editor? Or (c) you?[1]

○ Maybe it's because everyone is so overcommitted on their staffs, but the fact of the matter is, as we have seen, publishers are simply not very good at marketing books.

The result is that if you don't help market, you really will have no one but yourself to blame should the book's sales not meet your expectations.

Okay, where do you start?

Well, the first step is simply offering to help. Have your editor introduce you to the marketing and public relations (P.R.) people assigned to your book. (Someone is assigned to every book on the publisher's list.)

The marketing people will smile, tell you they are glad to meet you, and that they are "looking forward to working together." And then the moment you leave they will look heavenward and pray that they never see you again.

Their reaction is pretty easy to understand. At best, your offering to help is going to be seen by everyone in the marketing department as implied criticism of them. (If they were perfect at their jobs, they wouldn't need any help, would they?) And at worst, they are going to see you as a meddlesome busybody who doesn't know the first thing about marketing.[2]

---

1. And to be coldly mercenary about it, you could frame the multiple-choice question that we just discussed this way: Who stands to make the most money from your book's success? Someone who is on the publisher's staff or you, the person who is getting a royalty on every copy of your book that is sold?

2. And if you actually do know something about marketing, the marketing and public relations staffs at your publisher are going to be quick to point out that you don't know anything about *book* marketing, which they will contend (incorrectly) is a unique form of marketing and should be left to professionals—like them.

**Even with a big publisher behind you, the best
person to market your book is *you.***

Why then bother to offer to help? Because you want to work with
the sales, marketing, and public relations departments and not against
them, no matter what their initial attitude might be.

What can you do about that attitude? Nothing, at first. Acknowledge up front you are going to meet with some—and maybe a lot
of—resistance when you say you want to help.

But while you must accept their attitude—doing anything else will
be counterproductive—you don't have to let them control the agenda.

Instead of saying, "Let me know what I can do," and then being surprised when your phone doesn't ring, take the initiative. Offer to do the work. Be specific and start with easy wins. One place where you probably want to get involved is an area that doesn't even involve the marketing department. Some of these are discussed below.

Prefaces/Forewords/Afterwords

If *you* write an introduction, very few people are going to read it. If the head of the Mafia, Warren Buffett, or Jerry Seinfeld writes a foreword (or afterword) for you, it is a different matter.

If you can get a "name" to write something as part of your book, by all means do it.

For example, on *Customers for Life* we got Tom Peters, then at the height of his fame, to write the foreword and Stanley Marcus, of Neiman-Marcus and the godfather of upscale retailing, to do an afterword.

Drawing on star power helps. A lot.

Blurbs

One of the most effective forms of marketing is capitalizing on the credibility of someone else. (That, in essence, is what you are trying to do by having the foreword and/or afterword written by a so-called name.) **[E.K.: Of course, it's best to have all this nailed down *before* the book is announced in your publisher's catalog and its sales reps are trying to sell your book to their accounts.]** If a respected publication says nice things about your book, more people are likely to buy it. It is the same thing with blurbs (the quotes on the book jacket and/or on the first couple of pages of the book) where someone praises what you have written as the greatest thing since sliced bread and tells potential readers they would be darn fools not to memorize every word you have written.

Typically, the marketing department will ask you for the names of people whom they should contact to write those blurbs—both people you know and people you'd love to have say nice things about your book—and they will send first- or second-pass pages to them, along with a form letter asking for a blurb.

In addition, they will also send your book out to the usual suspects. If it's a marketing book, then whoever is the hot marketing guru of the moment will be asked to "blurb" your book; if a leadership book, someone who is on the cover of the business magazines all the time will be asked; and so forth.[3]

By following this approach, you will get some endorsements, but they will probably be as creative as the path that led to them—that is, not very.[4]

Why not take control of this process yourself? First off, you probably have better access to these people than the marketing department; second, you will be able to indicate directly what you would love the person to say; and third, it demonstrates to the marketing and

---

3. But they may not know why they are being asked.

My favorite example of that involved an internationally famous businessman, one whose name you'd instantly recognize. I went out to interview him for a magazine piece and noticed that his desk was partially covered by new books and galleys.

"Are you a big reader of business books?" I asked.

"Not really. But everybody seems to send them to me," he says. "I don't know why."

"Maybe they would like you to give them a blurb."

"I never thought of that," he said.

4. Why even bother then? Well, for one thing, okay blurbs are better than no blurbs at all. And for another, sometimes the universe will surprise you in a good way.

For example, on the book I did about coaching my son in Little League, I fantasized out loud about the possibility of getting a veteran baseball broadcaster to say nice things about *My Season on the Brink.*

Here's what Ernie Harwell, the longtime voice of the Detroit Tigers and a man who has called countless national games as well, had to say: "A delightful book. Paul has taken a unique approach to a universal problem: How to teach kids to play baseball and have fun too. I enjoyed every page."

Harwell, who wouldn't know me if I bumped into him on the street, responded to the standard letter from my publisher, St. Martin's. Ernie Harwell, who recently retired after about fifty-five years calling games, is a very nice man.

P.R. departments that you can be of help when it comes to marketing your book.[5]

Flap Copy

This is a much overlooked area where you can help.

The flap copy is the prose written on the inside of a hardcover's dust jacket that tells readers how wonderful your book is. While it occasionally contains blurbs, most often it is a simple description of what the book is about. And that is exactly the problem. It's too simple, too basic. Authors, editors, and publishers are missing a huge opportunity to sell the book.

Don't be another victim. Pay a lot of attention to the flap copy for your book.

In large part, potential book buyers *do* judge a book by its cover. Think about how *you* evaluate a book you don't know much about if

---

5. The following are some quick tips on blurbing:

1. More is better. Try to get every single person you can.
2. Relevance counts. Unless you can get the pope or the president of the United States to say nice things about you, you want the person giving the blurb to seem to be a logical endorser. If it is a leadership book, you want leaders endorsing it. And the more diverse the field, the better. Sure, try to get business folks, but why not a football coach, the head of a large church, an army general. After all, they are leaders, too.
3. Name recognition counts. If the person endorsing your book—such as Bill Gates or Oprah Winfrey—isn't instantaneously recognizable, go for endorsers who work for well-known companies. If people don't recognize the name of the endorser, or the firm they work for, you better have a darn good reason for expecting the blurb to have any impact.
4. Start early. Once you have a first draft of your manuscript, you can start sending it out.
5. Don't be shy. Invariably, someone will say, "What should I write?" Be sure to provide examples, stealing liberally from blurbs that you have seen elsewhere that impressed you. If someone asks you to write the blurb for them, by all means do it. Just make sure they see it and sign off on it before it pops up on your book jacket. (But whenever possible, get them to write it. Odds are they will be more enthusiastic than you would be writing for them.)

you pick it up in a bookstore. You spend a lot of time looking at the book jacket. Does the book have an intriguing title? (more on that in a second); who endorsed it (that is, who blurbed it?); what does the author look like?[6] **[E.K.: Keep in mind that blurbs are less important on paperbacks with no flaps; the publisher needs to leave room for "selling copy."]**

And then, if you are like me, you look at the flap copy and even start to read it.

If potential book buyers are going to take a look at it, you should spend some time working on what your flap copy says.

Traditionally, the editor writes the copy—or more likely the editorial assistant does. **[E.K.: For the record, Paul, but at AMACOM, it's actually a *copywriter* who writes the copy (another good reason to do a good job on your marketing questionnaire) and the acquisitions editor who line edits it.]** And while I am all in favor of twenty-three-year-old assistants who want to move up the publishing ranks getting as much experience as they can, I would like them to learn on someone else's time (and book). That's why I offer (repeatedly) to write the flap copy for my books.

The following is the flap copy I created for *Customers for Life*:

> "I cannot imagine any business or businessperson who could not benefit from this book. Hidden beneath the surface of these pages is nothing short of a full-blown theory of management and customer service. It could invigorate any enterprise."—Tom Peters[7]

---

6. If you don't see an author photo on the book jacket, odds are what you are missing is a picture of an unattractive writer.

7. If you have a big name supporting your book, lean on it heavily. When *Customers for Life* was published in 1990, there was no bigger name in the management heavens than Thomas J. Peters of *In Search of Excellence* fame. That is why his quote leads off the flap copy.

"If you don't learn from this book, it's your fault."—Stanley Marcus.[8]

Tom Peters and Stanley Marcus are saying what executives from P&G, Wal-Mart, Ford, and scores of other companies already know: Carl Sewell has learned how to turn one-time buyers into lifetime customers.[9, 10]

For Sewell, a lifetime customer will spend $332,000 at one of his 10 car dealerships. And, as Sewell points out in this straightforward guide to customer service, if you treat each customer as if he's worth that much money to you, you're bound to treat them better.

How? By smiling at them?[11]

Sure, in part. But, says Sewell, "The smiles, politeness, and being willing to go the extra mile are just the icing. The real cake is the systems that allow you to do a good job."

8. This quote is here because I love it. It is not something that would traditionally be included because (a) it follows a quote from Peters, and there is only so much space you have on the flap copy and "do you really want to have two quotes back to back?" and (b) it is too "in your face."

Tough. It's a great quote. And a great endorsement and so we fought successfully to keep it in.

9. By referencing big companies—all of which had at one point sent managers to visit Sewell—I was trying to trade off on both their companies' name recognition and implicit endorsements. The fact that the then-chairperson of Wal-Mart, David Glass, gave us an actual endorsement, in the form of a blurb that was featured prominently on the back cover, only strengthened this effect.

10. This sentence is here to drive home the point that we were going to deliver on the promise in the subtitle of the book: How to turn that one-time buyer into a lifetime customer. In business books, having a how-to component is vital, I truly believe. Managers may or may not like theory, but they love anything that will show them how to do their jobs better.

11. It doesn't hurt to directly take on whatever skepticism your book might face. The implicit premise of the book was that customer service is a business strategy. (I failed to state this explicitly either in the flap copy or in the book itself. At the time, there was no one treating customer service seriously. I was afraid by saying it directly we would scare people away. In retrospect, I was wrong.) People were going to doubt the whole idea. Given that, it seemed a good idea to confront their doubts right on the flap copy of the book, and that was as close as I came to taking on the issue directly.

In a series of short, well-focused chapters, Sewell explains how he created those systems and you can too.[12] He explains:

- ○ How to "under promise and over deliver"
- ○ How to see what the customer sees
- ○ How you can turn your employees into "service superstars"
- ○ How to communicate a readiness to serve
- ○ Why there is no such thing as "after hours"
- ○ The importance of measuring everything you do[13]

This is not a theoretical guide to customer service. It's a "how to" written by a practitioner who's developed an approach to customer service that works whether you offer inexpensive products or expensive ones.[14]

As Tom Peters says, "Sewell's approach to service will work equally well for companies big and small. I encourage you to dig in, chuckle, ponder, and take action now."[15]

12. In understanding why this sentence is here, it helps to remember what business books were like fifteen years ago. They still leaned heavily toward the academic. The last word you would use to describe them was "fun."

While I didn't think what we had created with *Customers for Life* was going to be as entertaining as an episode of *The Simpsons*, I did want to get across the point that what they were about to read was not going to be deadly dull and boring.

13. Looking back, this list could have, and should have, been stronger. The idea here was to write down some of the benefits you are going to provide to the reader. We have thirty-six chapters, each containing an idea that a reader could put to use immediately. I am not sure that I picked the six best. I was more worried about making the ideas fit on the book jacket.

14. You have to pound home the reason people NEED to buy your book. And this was also a chance to underscore that this book was designed for people working inside big companies and entrepreneurs running their own firms.

15. There is something to be said for symmetry. We began the flap copy with Tom Peters, and it just felt right to end it the same way. Besides, it is a great quote.

Catalog Copy

As long as you're doing the flap copy, suggest writing the catalog copy as well. [**E.K.: Not all publishers will receive these suggestions favorably, as you know.**]

As we mentioned before, publishers have specific selling seasons. For some it is two times a year, while for others, three. And still others have four. For each selling season—such as their spring list—they prepare a catalog where they try to put their books in the best possible light. The catalog goes to book retailers and reviewers (so they know which books to watch out for) at least four to six months before the books actually ship to the stores.

Editors typically write the catalog copy for each book they are responsible for. [**E.K.: Maybe at mass market houses, but not at any publishers where I've ever worked.**] If you volunteer to take the chore off their hands they will be grateful. [**E.K.: I wouldn't say that.**] They might even come to your defense when there is a push to change the title of your book. [**E.K.: Some editors will do that for you even if you *don't* butter them up.**]

The Name Game

Of the many things I don't understand about the way publishers do business, and as you learned by now that list is long, this is near the top of the list: Why don't publishers have a better system—heck, why don't they have *any* real system—for figuring out the best possible title for each book they publish?

When you pitched your book to an editor, it had a title. One you thought about fairly carefully before you put it on the first page. Woody Allen may call the current film he is writing and directing *The Current Woody Allen Movie* (which he does during the production process), but you gave your book a title that you liked, possibly even loved.

You might expect the book to be published under that title. But you would be wrong. In publishing, changing a book's title at the last minute—sometimes even after the catalog is printed—is about as common as an expense account lunch, which is another way of saying "very." [**E.K.: Actually, it's not too often changed after the catalog has been printed—and then it's usually because, as you point out next, the sales reps or the accounts HATE it. But yes, before that it happens routinely.**]

Why all the changes, especially at the last minute? Sometimes the editor gets a "brainstorm" at the proverbial eleventh hour. Sometimes the sales force comes back and says, "I tried the title out on some of my accounts and they don't like it."[16] And sometimes a member of the editorial board gets a "terrific" idea shortly before the book is scheduled to go to press.

But the reality is their opinions really are no better than yours. [**E.K.: Ahem. I beg to differ—especially since most authors of nonfiction books are neither writers by trade nor marketing people. By the way, Paul, why don't you tell readers your initial proposal title for this book? Wasn't it *What Color Shirts Do Your Readers Wear?* Fortunately, the author in you emerged with something slightly less abstruse while you were writing the manuscript.**] And since, as we talked about in Chapter 2, publishers don't conduct focus groups for titles, all they have when they suggest a new title is an opinion about what they think will sell more books. It is not based on anything more than "my longtime experience in this business." And to be kind, that longtime experience frequently doesn't add up to much. [**E.K.: I take exception to your kindness.**]

16. Now it may shock you to learn that a salesman is not above fibbing. If he doesn't like the title, he may invent some mythical customers who agree with his opinion that your title is awful. (He doesn't call those customers "me, myself, and I," but he could.) And then he lobbies long and hard for something he (and his "customers") like better, which coincidentally is often a title he—or those same mythical customers—have come up with.

But sometimes the customers do have a valid objection. For example, I originally called my second book *Marketing Stars*. Retailers, however, thought it would lead customers to believe I was writing about how to sell Tom Hanks or Meg Ryan, and not America's best marketing companies, and so the title became *Marketing Masters*. The retailers' concern might have been right. But the name change didn't help. As I've said, the book disappeared without a trace.

Sometimes they come up with a better title, sometimes they don't. Sometimes you can live with the change. But if you can't, it helps to have all the goodwill possible on your side within the publishing house.

The Sales Force

Pop quiz, hotshot. Who has the most power to make your book a success? The publisher's P.R. department? Well, it is a significant factor, sure. Reviewers? They can be important. But if the publisher's sales force doesn't get behind your book, the odds of you making the best-seller list are a whole lot longer.

In conjunction with every list the publisher puts out—spring, summer, or winter—there is a sales conference. While your editor will present your book in the best possible light to the sales troops, try to get yourself invited to speak as well. **[E.K.: Be prepared, though: Unless yours is what we call a "lead book," it's not likely you'll be invited.]** In fact, fight to get the chance to speak at the sales convention, or to talk to the sales force at one of their meetings that are held between sales conferences. **[E.K.: Don't be too discouraged if this doesn't work out; it's not generally an option.]**

The more the sales force knows about the book—and the more they like you—the harder they will work to sell it.[17]

Public Relations

Tom Peters gave me the best advice I have ever received when it comes to promoting a book: "Say yes to everything."

And that's why I have done Denver radio shows at 3 A.M. (fortunately I could do them from my home on the East Coast [where it was

---

[17.] There are also other sales meetings/conferences to be aware of. Book Expo is the national trade show for the publishing industry, and the worldwide meetings for the industry are always held annually in Frankfurt. The only way a publisher is going to think of inviting you to either one is if you have a HUGE book for them. However, if you are going to be in the area anyway—since publishers are not going to pay for the trip—see if you can get an invitation.

The moral: Take any and all opportunities to promote your book.

4 A.M.], so the only one who saw me constantly yawning was the dog). I was more than happy to sit for an interview with a weekly paper in South Dakota, and although I go to bed early, I gladly stayed up after midnight to do a three-minute Minneapolis television interview.

If someone asks, "Can you do an interview with . . ." the answer should always be YES.

You say yes to every interview request because you never know what it's going to take to get a snowball (sales of your book in this case) rolling downhill. [E.K.: **Also, remember that if you keep your publicist happy, for future interview opportunities she will call on** *you***—instead of another author who may be less cooperative.**]

True story. A senior vice president at IBM found himself stranded in the Pittsburgh airport when his connection was delayed. He wandered into a bookstore and picked up the recently published *Customers for Life* because he had caught a couple minutes of a radio interview Carl had done with an Oklahoma radio station the week before. (The guy traveled a lot.)

The vice president bought the book, read it during the flight, and liked it. He put it on the IBM recommended reading list that goes out to the corporation's hundreds of thousands of employees, some of whom picked it up and told their friends who worked at other companies, who told their friends, and five months after publication—an incredibly long time in publishing—we had a bestseller on our hands. This is why you do every interview possible.[18]

As for where those interviews will take place, if you know any-

---

18. Why, you may be wondering, would you ever be tempted to turn down an interview? There are a couple of reasons. Your publisher will try to schedule as many as possible in a short time frame surrounding when your book is published, and you could get tired—and tired of answering the same questions.

In addition, the fact that no interviewer will have read your book—and believe me, no one interviewing you will have read it—could make you cranky.

It doesn't matter what reason you have for not doing the interview; do the interview.

one at a media outlet—even if it is only the cable access show in your home town—be sure to mention it to the P.R. person assigned to your book.

If you don't know anyone, don't worry. Knowing whom to contact is actually one thing that most publishers' marketing departments are good at.

Reviewers

This is another area where publishers have traditionally done well. If you have written a book about television commercials, they will, as a matter of course, send it to *Advertising Age* and *AdWeek*. However, you may know of specialized media, especially in your field, that your publisher doesn't know about. By all means, when you are aware of these outlets tell the marketing department about these potential places to pitch your book. And take an extra thirty seconds to make sure that they send a review copy to the appropriate person at the publication/outlet, doubling your chances of getting a mention.

Doing More on Your Own

You can bring in an outside public relations/marketing firm to supplement the work of your publisher's people. There are, however, a couple of threshold problems in doing so.

The first problem, as mentioned before, is the expense, which can easily run $10,000 a month, with a minimum commitment of three months required. Second problem is the inherent resentment of your publisher's internal people. If they aren't crazy about your offer to help, can you imagine how they are going to be if an outside firm comes in? **[E.K.: Nonsense. Just because the publisher doesn't want to spend $30,000 doesn't mean they don't want *you* to! My dear, we *never* carp about an author who wants to spend his own money on promotion.]**

What can you do about this? Well, from the category of "if you don't ask, you don't get," see if your publisher will pay for bringing in outside help. (If he or she will, that will ease the internal resentment a bit. If the boss has sanctioned it, it can't be all bad, or probably more accurately it would be a bad career move to fight against it.)

Failing that, you might want to spend your time doing other things to generate sales, such as arranging speaking engagements.

Lining Up Speaking Gigs

Once, many years ago, I spent a very pleasant couple of hours at a hotel bar in San Francisco with syndicated humor columnist Art Buchwald, who explained to me that writing the column was a *loss leader* for him.

Now, I understood the term. It is applied to things like the milk or diapers that are sold in supermarkets at cost, or actually less than cost, to lure customers into the store, in the hopes that they buy other items (that have higher margins).

What I couldn't understand was how it applied to Buchwald's column.

"That's simple, kid," he said speaking out of the side of his mouth as he always does. "The column attracts them," he said, gesturing to the senior management of a company that had hired both Buchwald and me to speak, "and then they pay through the nose to get me to come talk to their convention." (Buchwald was getting about five times what I was to speak, and I thought I was getting paid a lot.)

You, too, can benefit from Buchwald's advice. The moment you have a signed contract, contact speaking bureaus, trade organizations, and industry conference organizers and offer your services as a speaker.

If they accept, you have a chance to be paid twice. First, the conference organizers will pay for your appearance, and second, you can sell a lot of books, by either having the organization buy them as part of your appearance or making them available to conference-goers at the event.[19]

Some people would argue that as long as they are buying books it is enough. You don't need to be paid for doing a speaking appearance. And you might feel that way. That's fine. But I don't. While it is true that you will be promoting your book at the event, it is also true you will be preparing a speech, traveling to the destination, attending the social events associated with the speech (such as the welcoming dinner or the farewell cocktail party), doing the speech itself, and then traveling home. For doing all that, I think you should be compensated over and above the books you sell. I charge for speeches. You don't have to.

How Will You Know When Your Marketing Efforts Are Successful?

One of the frustrating things about working this hard at marketing your book is that immediate feedback is hard to come by. The best proof that you have been successful comes in your royalty state-

---

19. The preferred way to do this is to have whomever is booking you for the event contact your publisher's special sales force—they are the people who handle bulk sales—and have your publisher sell the organization a bunch of books at a substantial discount.

The second preferred way is for your publisher to arrange to have a bookseller who has a store near where the event is being held handle the sales. Not only does that make the publisher's life easier, but the books the retailer sells count when publications are compiling bestseller lists. (Books sold at a substantial discount, that is, bulk sales, are not included when they are compiling the numbers.)

Now, as I said, those are the two preferred ways. And they are also the methods I have always followed. But there are some folks who buy massive numbers of books from their publisher—at up to an 80 percent discount off the cover price—and then sell the books themselves to the people they speak to. [**E.K.: 80 percent?! The key word in that sentence was *massive*.**]

No, the books they buy don't count toward the bestseller lists, but even if they sell the books for 50 percent off the cover, they have made a tidy profit. This is tacky, since it puts the author in competition with his or her publisher—and book retailers—but some authors do it. [**E.K.: It happens more often than you'd think, Paul— and actually, we have no problem with authors reselling their books at their speaking engagements.**]

ments from your publisher, and as we have seen, those statements can easily contain data that is ten months old. It might not be until the following April that you know how many books you sold between July and December of the previous year.

If you bug your editor enough, he or she will give you a rough idea of how well the book is doing. (Editors get periodic updates on sales.) [**E.K.: I wouldn't recommend bugging too often. Not good to alienate your editor (who also has hundreds of other authors who are curious about their sales figures too), since she's your point person and the one who will see to it that all your book-related problems get solved.**] But unless the book is taking off like the next John Grisham novel, the editor's reports will be vague, since they don't want to upset you. (Hearing you sold six books last week is bound to be depressing.)

The other way of checking is—as we mentioned before—going either to Amazon.com or BN.com and checking on your sales.

This is an easy way to tell if your marketing efforts are paying off or not.

If they are, swell. Keep plugging away. If they are not, *you* need to work harder.

CHAPTER 9

Going Your Own Way—Nontraditional Approaches to Being Published, or "Publisher? We Don't Need No Stinkin' Publisher"[1]

When I was a kid, I was always fascinated by the tiny advertisements that filled the back of the *New York Times* book review section every Sunday.

For the life of me, I have no idea why I looked at them. Maybe

---

1. With apologizes to B. Traven, who wrote the book *The Treasure of the Sierra Madre,* on which the movie of the same name, directed by John Huston, is based.

In the film, a band of Mexican bandits approaches Humphrey Bogart and crew (Walter Huston and Tim Holt) claiming to be federales. When Bogart asks to see their badges, the head of the band, played by Alfonso Bedoya, responds by saying, *"Badges? We ain't got no badges. We don't need no badges. I don't have to show you any stinking badges!"*

A very similar exchange existed in the book.

because it was the only part of the section I understood. The reviews were then (and remain now, to be honest) a bit too esoteric for my taste. But I understand the advertisements that are still there every Sunday and haven't changed much since I was a kid.

There were (and still are) advertisements for out-of-print books. And from people who would track down out-of-print books for you. (As a kid, I wondered why the people looking for out-of-print books didn't just contact the people who said they could find them.)

But the one advertisement I was always drawn to was for Vantage Press, which, I knew from growing up in and around Manhattan, was located in a less-than-terrific part of the city, west of Pennsylvania Station, somewhere near the Hudson River.

What was so appealing about the advertisement was simple: The people at Vantage Press promised to publish your book!

Or *my* book, as I thought about it as a kid.

I had no great desire to be a writer back then. Maybe it would be something to think about after I finished my stellar career playing third base for the New York Yankees, but I wasn't one of the people who always dreamed of being a writer. I wrote faster than any other kid I knew growing up—note I said faster, not better—but writing in and of itself had no appeal. It was just another form of homework that I had to get through, so I could go out and play baseball. The fact that I could get through it quickly was a plus, but that was about the only attraction writing had for me.

Still, I found the whole idea of getting a book published intriguing. I somehow knew that the advertisements for the Vantage Presses of the world were for "vanity" publishing, meaning that you had to pay to have your book printed, instead of having someone pay you for writing the book. And I also knew somehow that real authors, like the children's book illustrator who lived two floors below us in our apartment building, scoffed at the idea. But I never quite understood what was wrong with it.

The market has finally caught up to my perception—and self-publishing is now a plausible and strategically sound idea in a number of cases. But before we talk about the advantages of publishing a book on your own, and the situations where it could be appropriate, let's examine where the taint comes from.

Why Does Self-Publishing Have Such a Bad Name?

The answer to this question is simple: Until recently, most self-published books stank.

As Jerrold Jenkins, owner and founder of Jenkins Group, Inc., a Michigan-based publishing services provider that publishes books for people for a price, explained:

> Most of these books had no business seeing the light of day. By definition, the self-publishing process removes the checks and balances that major publishers provide by rejecting sub-standard manuscripts and "separating the wheat from the chaff." The explosion of print-on-demand publishing in the 1990s [which began with desktop publishing where software programs allowed anyone with a personal computer to produce a professional-looking book, and has evolved into an industry] exacerbated this problem, flooding the market with poorly written and edited books.
>
> Fortunately, most independent publishers [When Jenkins says "independent publisher," he's referring to what we think of as a "vanity press" or "subsidized publisher"] treat their craft like the serious business it is and create books only when they know there is a market for them. They use professional editing, layout, and design to produce products that can compete on the superstore shelves alongside books by mainstream publishers. These independent publishers have business and marketing plans to guide their projects and know what it takes to sell their books.

So, although there are still many self-published books that have no business being foisted on anyone, a significant percentage not only

look professional but also contain content that is of interest to someone other than the author and his or her immediate family.

Advantages of Going It Alone

Why go it alone? Well, the tradition of being self-published has a
long and noble history.[2] But beyond trying to be part of history, there
are four main reasons you may want to self-publish.

It's a Sure Thing

Some 60,000 books are published each year, and while nobody
keeps statistics, my guess is ten times that number, or 600,000 full-
blown ideas—that is, 600,000 formal book proposals—are rejected.
Some mistakenly so. If you publish the book yourself, you know it is
going to be a book; you don't need to have its fate determined by an
editor sitting in an office somewhere. (And, if you have been turned
down by traditional publishers, this is your chance to see your work
in finished form.)

Speed

As we have seen, it can take as long as a year from the time a manuscript is turned in until it reaches the bookstores. And this is on top of
the time it takes you to actually write the book.

For many people, and especially for many businesses that plan to
tie the book into their marketing efforts, that delay is simply unac-
ceptable. The material can grow stale in the two years or so it takes
from when you begin writing until the book is actually in bookstores.
[E.K.: Assuming you can get it in the brick-and-mortar stores without a traditional publisher.] This is especially true if you're writing
about anything that has a technology component, because a major
marketing opportunity could be lost. If you publish the book on your
own, it can be completed in a couple of months, excluding writing

2. And includes writers such as Mark Twain, Edgar Allan Poe, and Stephen Crane.

time. You will be amazed how the amount of time it takes to write your book shrinks when you know that the absolute second you are done, you can move the book into production.

Control

Want to see an author turn beet red? Ask her about how much input she had about what the cover of her book looked like. Or how it was marketed. Or even what the book was called. (All these things are discussed in detail in Chapter 6.)

If you publish yourself, you have the freedom to make all the decisions concerning the direction of your project. You ultimately have the final say regarding all aspects of your book's development, look, and feel. Plus, you will be able to direct all the promotional efforts. In short, you—and not a publisher—have total control over your book project.

For example, many authors' books are produced as marketing tools for themselves or their products. If you are publishing yourself, you can make the book a 200-page commercial if you want to. Who would read such a thing would be another matter, but the fact is the book will read exactly the way you want; there is no third party "interference" from a publisher "suggesting" changes to the manuscript.[3]

Also, you decide when it goes out of print. A publisher can simply (without any consultation with you) decline to print more copies, because the ones in print haven't sold fast enough. And he can have that decision forced on him by retailers, some of whom give new books only six weeks to prove themselves. If they are not racking up significant sales by then, the retailer ships the books back to the publisher for a full refund.

If you are publishing the book, you can keep printing copies until the cows come home.

And, if you want to sell your book to a traditional publisher at any time, you can.

---

3. This is not as silly as it first sounds. Suppose you want to include a book along with the purchase of a new car, spa, or other high-ticket product someone buys from you. You can custom-tailor the book to support the purchase either to extol the features of what they have just bought or to serve as a glossy customer-service manual.

This is no small point. As the subsidy publishers will tell you, there are many books that began life being self-published only to find a home later with a traditional publisher.[4] [**E.K.: It should be noted, though, that if the book was not a big seller and has already gotten its fair share of publicity, publishers may be reluctant to take it on.**]

Why this happens is not hard to explain.

The author writes a proposal—or perhaps, mistakenly, the entire book—and sends it out to countless traditional publishers. They reject it, but undeterred he has the book printed and begins selling it on his own.

If the book takes off, one of two things can happen. A traditional publisher will come calling with checkbook in hand and offer to buy all the rights to the book. Or you can take a history of your sales to all the publishers who turned you down the first time.

Why will they listen to you now? That's simple. You have a track record. You have sold X,000 or XX,000 books, so there is no longer a question of whether the book will sell. It has sold. The only question is how many more copies can a traditional publisher sell for you.[5]

---

4. Among the best known are:

- O *What Color Is Your Parachute*—the job hunting guide by Richard Nelson Bolles, which was eventually sold to Ten Speed Press, has sold over 8 million copies.
- O *The Celestine Prophecy*—the spiritual and self-discovery adventure, originally self-published by James Redfield, was eventually acquired by Warner Books.
- O *The Christmas Box*—the story of a struggling family and a wealthy widow by Richard Paul Evans that was ultimately acquired by Simon & Schuster.

5. Can you continue to sell the book on your own, even if you give the rights to a traditional publisher? Maybe. Under terms of the contract the publisher will have you sign, you won't be able to sell into the same channels—so that will eliminate retailers both big, like Barnes & Noble, and small, like your mom-and-pop local bookstores. And it will also place online retailers like Amazon.com off limits.

However, you may be able to continue to sell through your own Web site, if you have been doing that, and as part of your speaking engagements.

This raises the obvious point of comparing what a publisher can do for you versus what you can do on your own. If you think you can do better without a traditional publisher behind you, then by all means don't relinquish any of the rights.

Times Have Changed

Five years ago, I never would have included this chapter. After all, traditional publishers have the advantage of an established distribution network, and having a major publisher bringing your book to the marketplace gives it serious credibility.

But these factors are less critical today and can be overcome. Independent distributors, such as Ingram and Baker & Taylor, will be happy to try to get you into bookstores; they don't care who pays them—you, or the people who run Simon & Schuster **[E.K.: Of course, the good folks at Simon & Schuster and other publishers may have a few of their *own* people whose job it is to get their books into stores. . . .]**—and the credibility issue, although important, is becoming less and less of a factor.

As more and more media spring up, we are becoming accustomed to receiving information from nontraditional sources. And if a Web site or a publishing house we have never heard of (You, Inc.) provides us with helpful information, we, as consumers, are happy. The publisher's pedigree is still important—it is like any other brand name; it stands for consistency and reliability—but it is less important than the content.

So, I think the taint associated with self-publishing is fading, especially when you publish a book aimed at a niche market.

Here's my favorite example: A friend of mine runs a research company that focuses on learning everything it possibly can about the high end of the market—people who buy Lexus cars, live in large homes, and are likely to send their kids to private schools.

The market for a book about how to conduct focus groups involving these people is incredibly small. Maybe, if you look hard enough, you could find 15,000 people worldwide inside advertising agencies and companies like Tiffany's who truly need the information my friend has learned over the past twenty years in business.

No traditional publisher is going to bring out a book that has such limited potential.

However, the potential market for the book is made up of people who really do need the information, and they are willing to pay for it.

You may well be able to forgo bookstore sales completely if you have a ready market of buyers within your niche. Marketing a book to a niche audience is much simpler and cheaper than marketing to the public at large.

My friend produced a small book that he is selling on his own—mostly through his company's Web site—at $275 a copy. Sales are not what you would call overwhelming. He is probably moving 250 copies a year. But that still adds up to about $70,000 of annual revenue, and once you subtract the marketing, printing, and fulfillment costs, it works out to about $50,000 before taxes. You'd be hard-pressed to find many authors who are getting that much in royalties each year.

What Does It Take to Independently Publish a Book?

With the independent—that is, self-publishing—model, there are countless variations your project might take, depending on the size and scope of what you are trying to accomplish. But if you're just getting started, it's likely you will be doing it all yourself.

I'll divide the task into two parts, actually producing the book and then selling it. Let's look at the production side first.

Writing, Copyediting, and Getting the Thing Printed

Unlike when you go the traditional route, if you decide to self-publish, you can start on the book immediately. There is no need for a proposal. That makes the process a little bit easier, but it may be the only place it does.

When you turn in your book to a traditional publisher, the company will perform certain functions for you. Someone will:

○ Edit what you have written, seeing that what you have written makes sense and that everything is in the right order

○ Copyedit what you have written, checking for spelling, punctuation, and grammar errors

○ Design the cover and the book's interior

○ Print your book

These are all things you will have to pay for, or do yourself, if you decide to self-publish.

On the Business Side

Besides being the author and publisher, you are also the financier, business manager, and promoter (not to mention collection agent, customer service representative, and shipping clerk). You must perform all these functions or hire someone to do them for you. [**E.K.: Paul, let's not overlook that a traditional publisher can also sell books internationally, and can make the author a nice piece of change by brokering the lucrative sales of translation rights, whose proceeds are generally split evenly between the author and publisher.**] Again, these would be tasks a traditional publisher would handle, but since you are going off on your own, these tasks are your responsibility.

Clearly, though, the biggest issue you need to address is the promotion of your book. To be successful, you need to think about marketing your book as you would any other product. In this instance, marketing can be boiled down to figuring who you would want to buy your book and what you need to do to get them to reach for their wallets. So, in your case that means you must do the following:

○ Define the target audience

○ Recognize the competition

○ Understand the market

○ Develop and realize your goal, through careful planning and determined action

"Of course, many services are available for hire, and it makes sense to enlist experts to handle the tasks you're least qualified for, don't enjoy, or simply don't have time to do yourself," says Jerrold Jenkins, whose company helps authors self-publish. "Regardless of how much of your project you subcontract, publishing independently requires a huge commitment of time and energy. Especially when the time comes to promote, you must be willing to 'live' your book, tirelessly selling it— and yourself. The old adage goes: When the author stops selling, the book stops selling. And that adage is absolutely right."

The Dollars and Sense of Self-Publishing

Okay, so what is it going to cost?

Well, if you print a bunch of books that you plan to sell on your own, the following table will give you some ballpark figures for a typical nonfiction publishing project:

What's It Gonna Cost?			
Book length in pages	Number of copies printed	Cost* Hardcover	Softcover
176[6]	5,000	$33,000	$20,000
256	5,000	$38,000	$25,000
328	5,000	$42,500	$30,000

SOURCE: The Jenkins Group, Inc.
*The estimates include editing, proofreading, cover design, text design and layout, printing, and registrations.

Jenkins advises his clients that if they have a ready market for 2,500 books through an established client base, speaking engagements, or special sales deals, the chance for success is great, and that, generally speaking, your break-even point is 1,500 books.

With a second printing of the same book, your cost per copy drops

6. What happens if you want to write a smaller book? Obviously, it will cost less. For example, if you purchase 5,000 copies of a 6x9, 125-page hardcover, it will cost you about $20,000 for professional editing, design and layout, and production, all conducted by a company such as Jenkins's.

from $4 to less than $2—because all the editing and layout costs have been paid for—so profits can go even higher.

Selling

Okay, you now have a printed book; where are you going to sell it? Well, there is a cliché in the publishing business that is absolutely correct; it goes: "Bookstores are the worst place to sell books."

And that is true. First, even if the bookstore agrees to carry your book, it is only going to stock a finite number, like two.[7] Second, you must cut the bookstore in on the profits—remember, the store is going to expect to get half the cover price—and third, the store won't go out of its way to push your book. It has is no reason to. The store doesn't care whether it sells your book or somebody else's; it is all the same. That puts the onus on you to promote the book and work hard on direct sales. That's where you sell in bulk to a group or organization. And it is also where the real profits are, because:

(a) You don't need to split revenues with distributors or retailers, because you are handling the sale yourself.

(b) Your fulfillment costs are less. You aren't shipping books out one at a time, but in bulk.

How do you handle these kinds of sales? There are numerous options:

○ You bundle the book into your speaking fee.

○ You sell the book to your trade association; many organizations, especially the larger ones, make books available to their members.

---

7. Again, this is not hyperbole. The number of copies bookstores keep of individual books has been steadily declining through the years. In the 1980s, you might find five copies of your book in stock. Now, you are lucky if they have two. It is not so much that they are carrying more titles—and so are reducing the number they carry of each—rather, they are using the space that used to go to books to sell higher-margin items, everything from coffee to greeting cards.

○ You arrange for someone to use what you have as a premium, fund-raiser, whatever. ("Sign up now and receive . . .")

Authors of traditional books always blame their publisher if sales are slow. If you publish on your own, you have no one to blame but yourself.

Should You Become a Pod Person?

There is one more variation to talk about for self-publishing, and that is print-on-demand (POD).

The concept is similar to the traditional self-publishing model, but in this case, instead of ending up with a garage full of books, you end up with a file—containing your book—that is located on an e-publisher's Web site. A customer (or you) can order a book at any time. Only then is the file downloaded and printed in either hard or soft cover. The books are printed only on the demand, hence the name.

If you are a publisher, the nice thing about POD is that it eliminates three of the biggest costs in publishing—warehousing, large print runs (yes, the cost per book drops the more you print, but the total cost increases), and returns (when all those books don't sell). That is great for the companies that print on demand, but it doesn't do much for you, the author of what they are printing.

The electronic publishers will assist you—to a limited extent—in designing your book, and most will help with editing, copyediting, and marketing for an additional fee.

The biggest advantage of going this route is cost. It can take as little as $100 to get your book "published."

The biggest disadvantage (beside the fact that you have to pay for getting your book published) is that there is a cap on what you can make. Authors are paid royalties that range—depending on which POD publisher you are doing business with—between 20 percent and 30 percent. Given the cost savings of their business models—and the fact that you are paying them to get the book published—you might have expected the payout to be higher. [E.K.: **Yes, if you did your** own subsidiary rights deal, you'd keep all the money—but, again, publishers split most of their subsidiary rights income fifty-fifty, and if you're publishing yourself, it's tough to make your own deals—for e-rights, translation rights, etc.]

Should You Do It?

Self-publishing is definitely an option. Like many decisions in life, it is a question of cost versus benefit. If you think publishing this way is the most expeditious (which it almost always is) and most potentially profitable (possibly), and a traditional publisher's pedigree is either not an option (they said no) or not worth the price (they keep most of the profits), then this is something you should look at very seriously.

But recognize going in all the potential downsides—the cost, the work you will have to do yourself; the fact that distribution is harder to come by [E.K.: **especially overseas**] and reviews may be nonexistent.[8] Weigh the upside—the book is guaranteed to be a book and guaranteed to appear exactly the way you want—against the negatives and make your decision.

---

8. Reviewers are inundated with books to review. Self-published books are the first to be moved to the "no" pile, because so many of them are bad, and their distribution is frequently less than universal.

In this day and age, anyone can publish a book.
In other words, "You don't need no stinkin' publisher."

Does This Describe You?

The whole idea for this book started with a working dinner designed to discuss magazine features I could write. Who knew what it would become?

To put the idea's genesis into perspective, you can look at the following draft of a piece that was written to run in Inc. *magazine. While it never did, it will give you an idea of what can happen if you say yes, when a friend asks you to do him a favor.*

Are You Sure Hemingway Started Like This?

Q: What do you get when you offer to send *Inc.* readers a memo about "how to get your book published"?

A: Overwhelmed.

BY PAUL B. BROWN

It began as these things often do:

I'm having dinner with the editor and executive editor of this magazine—I am trying to drum up work, they are looking for a reason to write off a fine meal on their most-impressive expense accounts—and in passing I mention a telephone call I received that day.

"The head of P.R. for X (a *major* New York bank) said his CEO wants to do a book and they need a ghostwriter. The P.R. guy asked what the process was for creating a book and getting it published is like. So, I e-mailed him the memo I send everyone and . . ."

"The memo? What memo?" the executive editor asks.

(The editor is busy studying the side of the wine list where prices send chills down the spines of mere mortals. We ignore him.)

"I get these calls all the time," I explain. "People always want to know what is involved in writing a book. It takes about an hour to describe the process in enough detail so that they'll know whether or not they want to go through it. So, to save some time, I wrote it all down. The memo is about twenty pages long."

"Can I see it?" the executive editor asks.

(The editor is talking to the sommelier. After an intense three-minute discussion, they agree on an Italian red that is priced as if Sophia Loren picked each grape by hand and then lovingly stomped every one individually with her bare feet.)

"Sure. I'll send you a copy when I get home tonight."

That was back in the fall. Excerpts of the memo ran in the February 2002 issue, along with an editor's note that said if, after reading the piece, you wanted the full memo, just let me know.

After the memo was printed, I received:

- A total of 778 e-mail requests for the complete memo

- Scores of follow-up telephone calls from people

- One additional meal with *Inc.*'s editors

Here's what I have learned.

There Are a Lot of Unhappy People out There and Many Are Working at Companies Both Big and Small

I had expected the notes from employees of Nabisco, IBM, and the Big Five accounting firms who told me they wanted to chuck it all and become writers. But most of the people who wrote that they were thinking of making a career change—and not thinking about "just" writing a book in their spare time—worked for small companies. Many of them ran *Inc.*-sized companies. Maybe they believed the lie "I'll start my own company; that way I will have control over my life" and are only now learning the truth.

Writers Really Have No Life

Other than lawyers, the largest group of people who asked for the memo were people who identified themselves as professional writers. It just goes to prove something that editors have known all along: Writers will do anything to avoid writing—even asking for a silly memo (or asking to mooch a nice meal).

As Julie Keller Learned in Eleventh Grade, If You Give Something Away for Free, You Become Very Popular

I knew people would write. But I couldn't have predicted that the *Boston Globe* would mention the article—triggering more requests—and that writers everywhere would post it on what seemed to be countless chat boards for authors, thus triggering more responses. (Which proved the previous point, I guess, about writers looking for ways to put off writing.) Of the 700-plus copies of the memo I sent out, only about half could be directly traced back to the *Inc.* article.

Secrecy

Experienced entrepreneurs will tell you that there is one sure tip-off for spotting a newbie. They are paranoid about revealing *anything* about their potential idea. But as experienced entrepreneurs know, ideas are commodities. It is the execution that counts.

It is no different when it comes to books. Anyone can say, "I have an idea for a horror story set in Maine." Stephen King gets millions for executing it well.

Still, most fledgling writers, like most fledgling entrepreneurs, refused to part with any info about their idea—even when they called me up and asked for help. That led to me getting a handful of snotty e-mails. (Read on for details.)

Agents

This one was my own damn fault. In the *Inc.* article and the complete memo, I promised to provide people with a list of agents. (My thought was maybe my own agent could sign a few new authors and perhaps I would finally get a Christmas present from him instead of just a card.) The problem was no one would tell me what their book idea was and so I couldn't match agent to idea. Unlike some panty hose, when it comes to agents, one size does not fit all. Some agents handle only certain genres like sci-fi or romance, others (like my agent) only nonfiction. But if I didn't know what someone wanted to write, I couldn't make a worthwhile recommendation, and just providing a generic list—"Here are some agents"—wouldn't have done anyone much good. (Sending my agent a tender coming-of-age story is like putting a steak in front of my ninety-pound yellow Labrador retriever; it will be ripped to shreds in a matter of seconds.)

But a promise is a promise. And so when (secretive) people wrote and said, "Give me the list of agents you promised," I did the best I could. Here's what I e-mailed back to them. (You will recognize the advice; it is what we talked about in Chapter 3).

Dear (Closed-Mouth Person):

Without knowing in detail what you want to write, who your market is, how you plan to address it—i.e., all the questions your proposal will answer in detail—a list of agents wouldn't help you much. Some agents are better at some things than others. The "secret" is to find a good match.

The easiest thing to do? Pick up a couple of books that are similar to the one you plan to write, see who the author thanks as his agent, and write that agent.

That way you are:

(a) Dealing with a qualified agent. (He sold a book.)

(b) Writing to someone who has an interest in your topic. (After all, he got a book in this area published.)

That satisfied most of the people. But I did get a couple of e-mails back that said: "So, no list of agents, huh? I guess I shouldn't have expected it."

Speaking of a Lack of Manners

Only 20 percent or so of the people who got the memo said, "Thanks." Women were far more polite than men, according to my very unscientific survey.

The Persistence of Youth

My return e-mails contained my office and cell phone numbers. In two separate incidents, a twenty-something—one in Chicago, the other in Texas—called both numbers every fifteen minutes until they finally reached me. Both wanted to skip the middleman (me) and deal directly with my agent, Rafe Sagalyn, convinced he would take them on as clients the moment he heard what they planned to write.

Unless I get a belated Christmas present soon, I may just give them Rafe's home number.

There Ain't No Shortcuts

Perhaps the biggest surprise I had was that only six people—less than 1 percent of the total number of folks who asked for the memo—wrote back to see copies of proposals. As I explained in the *Inc.* piece, in the complete memo (and earlier in this book), the proposal is *the key* to getting a book published.

The reason is simple. Editors don't want to read an entire book in order to figure out if they want to buy it. (And you don't want to write a book that no one will buy.) Hence, the importance of the proposal.

(As we talked about in Chapter 5, at its most basic level, a proposal is an outline of the book, which also serves as a multilevel marketing document.)

In the proposal—which usually runs between thirty and fifty pages—you explain what the book is about, why you are the best person to write it, and why the publisher is destined to make lots of money by betting on you. In other words, it is a serious sales pitch.

But the proposal also serves two other functions. It is the marketing document the editor will use to get the approval of the editorial board. That's important because editors only have the authority to buy you lunch, not give you a big advance. It also will double as the battle plan the publisher's marketing department will follow to move a lot of units.

So you can understand why it is important. What I can't understand is why people didn't ask for copies of proposals I've done that could serve as a template. But then, again, I don't understand why semiserious golfers don't practice their putting as much as all other parts of their game combined. During the average round, putts make up 50 percent of your shots.

Signers

Most e-mail programs let you create a static message that appears at the bottom of everything you send. It's where I (and a lot of people) put their address and telephone number. But some people use the spots to show some flare. The two favorites out of all the e-mails I received? A six-line quote from Martin Luther King Jr. poetically inspiring all of us to do our best at all times and the one from "Andrea: Modern wage slave by day, romance thriller writer by night."

About the Book Ideas Themselves

There were only a couple of surprises. Someone wanted to write about nineteenth-century English chimney sweeps—hey, I saw *Mary Poppins*; I'm a big Dick Van Dyke fan; maybe I can help him hook up with an editor—and there were a couple of people who wanted to write true coming-of-age stories. But the few people who actually talked about what they wanted to write stuck pretty close to home. Techies wanted to write computer books, human resources people wanted to write about their specialty, and so forth.

Was It an Advertisement for Myself?

If I had a nickel for everyone who wrote me to say: "What a clever idea publishing your memo in *Inc.* You are bound to get a dozen book deals out of it, with people calling you up to help them with their book," I'd have forty-five cents. No one has hired me—although the nice people at AMACOM have asked me to turn the memo into a book.

So that's what I have learned. If you missed the memo first time around, just send me an e-mail at paulbbrown@aol.com. Who knows? Maybe I'll get another meal out of the deal. Last time, the wine was very good.

Index

About the Author, Illustrator, and Editor

Paul B. Brown is the author, coauthor, or ghostwriter of more than twenty books, which have sold more than two million copies worldwide. A former writer and editor for *Business Week, Financial World, Forbes*, and *Inc.*, Brown spends seven days a week writing and throwing tennis balls to Buster, the world's tallest Labrador retriever.

Britton Payne is the author and illustrator of *Dumped* and *Laid Off,* the first two in his series of "little books to make you feel a little better." He has animated, directed, and written in New York City, but his next production will be attending law school. You can find out more about him and his work at www.brittonpayne.com.

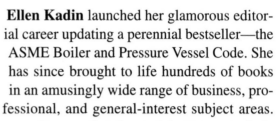

Ellen Kadin launched her glamorous editorial career updating a perennial bestseller—the ASME Boiler and Pressure Vessel Code. She has since brought to life hundreds of books in an amusingly wide range of business, professional, and general-interest subject areas. Rumors that she participates wantonly in each book she publishes are unfounded.

7755